THE ACTS OF THE APOSTLES

READING AND INTERPRETING THE BIBLE SERIES

THE ACTS OF THE APOSTLES

RICHARD P. THOMPSON

f·

THE FOUNDRY
PUBLISHING®

The Foundry Publishing®
PO Box 419527
Kansas City, MO 64141
thefoundrypublishing.com

ISBN: 978-0-8341-4173-5

Cover design: Caines Design
Interior design: Jody Langley

Unless otherwise indicated, all Scripture quotations are from the Holy Bible, New International Version® (NIV®). Copyright © 1973, 1978, 1984, 2011 by Biblica, Inc.™ Used by permission of Zondervan. All rights reserved worldwide. www.zondervan .com. The "NIV" and "New International Version" are trademarks registered in the United States Patent and Trademark Office by Biblica, Inc.™

Scripture quotations marked AT are the author's translations.

The following version of Scripture is in the public domain:
The King James Version (KJV)

The following copyrighted versions of Scripture are used by permission:
The Common English Bible (CEB). © Copyright 2011 Common English Bible. All rights reserved.

The New American Standard Bible® (NASB®), copyright © 1960, 1971, 1977, 1995, 2020 by The Lockman Foundation. All rights reserved.

The New Revised Standard Version Updated Edition (NRSVue). Copyright © 2021 National Council of the Churches of Christ in the United States of America. All rights reserved worldwide.

The Revised Standard Version (RSV) of the Bible, copyright 1946, 1952, 1971 by the Division of Christian Education of the National Council of the Churches of Christ in the United States of America. All rights reserved.

Library of Congress Cataloging-in-Publication Data

A complete catalog record for this book is available from the Library of Congress.

The internet addresses, email addresses, and phone numbers in this book are accurate at the time of publication. They are provided as a resource. The Foundry Publishing® does not endorse them or vouch for their content or permanence.

Contents

Introduction 7

Part I: Reading and Interpreting Acts – Selected Issues 9

    1. Influences in Reading and Interpreting Acts 11

    2. Reading and Interpreting Acts as a Narrative 31

Part II: Reading and Interpreting Selected Texts from Acts 41

    A. Speeches in Acts: Introduction 43

    3. What Got into *Him?* Peter's Pentecost Speech
      (Acts 2:14-36) 47

    4. An Unappreciated/Explosive Speech: Stephen's
      Jerusalem Speech (Acts 7:2-53) 57

    B. Summaries in Acts: Introduction 67

    5. Must I Tell You *Everything?* The Pentecost and Postarrest
      Summaries (Acts 2:42-47; 4:32-37) 71

    C. Characterization in Acts: Introduction 81

    6. Philip and the Ethiopian Eunuch: Perspectives about
      Believers and the Church (Acts 8:26-40) 85

    7. "Who's That Knocking at the Door?": Peter, Rhoda,
      and the Jerusalem Prayer Meeting (Acts 12) 99

    D. Repetition in Acts: Introduction 109

    8. Saul's/Paul's Encounter with Jesus . . . in Triplicate
      (Acts 9, 22, 26) 113

9. Cornelius and Peter, Told Over and Over Again
(Acts 10-11, 15) 123

E. Differences between Acts and the Pauline Letters:
Introduction 135

10. The Acts 15 Account of the Jerusalem Council
in Comparison to Galatians 1–2.......................... 139

11. "Say It Ain't So!": Paul and the Accusations against
Him (Acts 21) 153

Bibliography 167

Introduction

Books, like their authors and readers, may be said to have personalities. That is, they have their own characteristics, profiles, and even quirks. And this book is no different. On the one hand, it is part of the Reading and Interpreting the Bible Series from the Foundry Publishing, meaning that this book joins others in the series to assist readers in the understanding and use of appropriate methods of biblical interpretation. On the other hand, this book has a unique focus. Since the books in this series give attention to different genres, this work focuses on specific issues of the narrative genre in interpreting the book of Acts.

This volume is divided into two parts. The first part includes two chapters covering the general issues of reading and interpreting Acts. The second part includes nine additional chapters illustrating the interpretation of selected passages of Acts. These chapters are divided further by distinct characteristics: speeches, summaries, characterization, repetition, and differences between Acts and the Pauline Letters. Each of these characteristics is introduced by a brief introduction. The introduction offers some (not all) suggestions for the reading and interpretation of Acts before exploring the specific characteristic in a representative passage (or two).

Let me add a personal note to conclude this introduction. I have been blessed to have the book of Acts shape my life since Bible-quizzing days in high school. Little did I realize then that it would become my life's work, resulting in many articles on Acts, study notes about Acts for a study Bible, a translation of Acts for the Common English Bible project, a commentary on Acts, and now this book. I am amazed how this one book has continued to offer fresh words about God's will for us as God's people, God's church. May these sacred words of Scripture truly be God's word for you as you read and interpret (and pray over) Acts!

—Richard P. Thompson

August 2023

PART I

REST AND INTERPRETING ACTS—SELECTED ISSUES

1

Influences in Reading and Interpreting Acts

The task of reading and interpreting the book of Acts never happens in isolation. Like other books of the Bible, readers of Acts have interpreted it alongside other biblical texts. But the book of Acts, which is also known as the Acts of the Apostles, has had numerous interpretive and literary companions since it first appeared among the earliest believers. Very early in its existence and prior to its inclusion within the collection of the New Testament canon, the book circulated with the collection of General Epistles. Thus Acts was associated particularly with writings that were attributed to Peter and James, two significant characters within its narrative and among the first leaders within the early church.

Later and more recently, because of its canonical position preceding the Pauline corpus, the book has often functioned as a historical introduction to those letters. For instance, readers have often understood the description of Paul's ministry in the Greek city of Corinth—found in Acts 18—as useful historical background for their interpretations of Paul's letters to the Corinthians. But in the process, such readings have sometimes inadvertently relegated Acts into a secondary role, since the book has been valued as offering mere historical background for other biblical texts that have been read and interpreted for their theology and biblical message but has not been valued *for its own theological contributions and message* for the church and the Christian faith.

But other developments have accentuated the place and importance of Acts within the New Testament. Because of a common addressee and other extensive similarities (vocabulary, style, characterization, themes, etc.) between the Gospel of Luke and the book of Acts, the use of the title "Luke-Acts" reflects a general contemporary consensus about these two New Testament books: that they were originally written as a single literary work of two separate volumes.[1] This view about the Third Gospel and Acts has been largely assumed for the better part of a century, despite the separation of these two books in the Bible and the lack of any surviving manuscript or canonical list that connects them together.

The canonical separation of Acts from the Lukan Gospel corresponds with the lack of external evidence (i.e., evidence outside of the text of Acts) that might indicate that these two books are companion volumes of a larger work by a single author. Early usage of the Gospel of Luke and the Acts of the Apostles in the church shows these books were not read *together* but *separately*.[2] Despite their similarities, the differences in materials between these two books are significant and are reflected in their respective canonical locations. On the one hand, the Gospel of Luke focuses on the life of Jesus and is placed with two other similar (Synoptic) Gospels. On the other hand, the book of Acts focuses on the movements of the earliest believers, including Peter (chs. 1–12) and Saul/Paul (chs. 13–28). The canonical position of Acts before New Testament letters that largely address early Christian communities of faith corresponds with the general contexts described within that book.

However, these differences in canonical placement, materials, and usage still do not conceal the obvious literary connections between the Third Gospel and Acts. Both books address a common recipient named Theophilus (see more under "Addressee or Audience," p. 18). The book of Acts reminds Theophilus

---

1. See Henry J. Cadbury, *The Making of Luke-Acts* (New York: Macmillan, 1927).

2. See Andrew F. Gregory, *The Reception of Luke and Acts in the Period before Irenaeus: Looking for Luke in the Second Century*, Wissenschaftliche Untersuchungen zum Neuen Testament 2. Reihe 169 (Tübingen, DEU: Mohr Siebeck, 2003).

about the author's "first book" about Jesus (Acts 1:1, NRSVue), which is a likely reference to the Gospel of Luke. The extensive overlap in material between Luke 24 and Acts 1 links the two books together in multiple ways: "the promise of my [or the] Father" (Luke 24:49; Acts 1:4, RSV), the description of Jesus's followers as "witnesses" and the declaration that they would soon receive "power" to be said witnesses (Luke 24:48-49; Acts 1:8), and the emphasis on Jesus's ascension (Luke 24:51; Acts 1:9-11), among others. Although some differences between the two chapters also exist (e.g., the stories of Luke 24 could have transpired within twenty-four to forty-eight hours in contrast to the forty days of Acts 1), the general emphases of these chapters parallel one another. Also, descriptions of characters in Acts (e.g., believers) often mirror characters in the Lukan Gospel (especially Jesus). The abundance of such internal (literary) connections between these two books provides sufficient reason for reading them *together* rather than *separately*, despite the shortage of external evidence for doing so.

> **Readers should read and interpret both Luke's Gospel and Acts differently because of their place and function within that larger work of Luke-Acts.**

The decision to approach Acts as the second part of the larger, multivolume work "Luke-Acts" rather than treat it as a separate, distinct work leads to some important interpretive implications. First, readers should look for *primary* intertextual connections (i.e., connections *between* texts) between Acts and *the Gospel of Luke* rather than between Acts and *the Pauline Letters* (or the other Gospels). Because the broader literary world to which the book of Acts belongs includes the Lukan Gospel rather than the Pauline Letters, readers should remain cognizant of the ways *this* Gospel sets the literary or narrative stage for what happens in Acts.

Second, readers should read and interpret both Luke's Gospel and Acts differently because of their place and function within that larger work of Luke-Acts.

On the one hand, the reading and the interpretation of the Gospel of Luke are affected because *this* Gospel does not conclude with Jesus's resurrection (explicitly or implicitly; see Mark 16:1-8) or appearance among his followers, as do the other canonical Gospels (see Matt. 28:16-20; John 21:1-23). In fact, Luke's Gospel does not even end with Jesus's ascension, a unique feature among the New Testament Gospels (Luke 24:50-51). Rather, the hopeful description of Jesus's followers who returned in worship to Jerusalem anticipates something more (see vv. 52-53). On the other hand, the Acts narrative presumes the specific story of Jesus as it unfolds in the Third Gospel. That is, it is not just the *story of Jesus* but the *Lukan story of Jesus* that the book of Acts supposes to be on the minds of its readers as they themselves witness within the latter narrative those who serve as witnesses to Jesus's resurrection.

Third, the Gospel of Luke and the Acts of the Apostles *together* create the largest *single* contribution to the New Testament. Such a work is noteworthy on several levels. This single work focuses on the longest time span of any New Testament work, extending from just before the announcement of Jesus's birth to Paul's house arrest and ministry in Rome (about sixty-five years). Thus, from a chronological perspective, it offers a more extended perspective of God's purposes through Jesus Christ and among God's people, both *(a)* in leading up to the crucifixion, resurrection, and ascension of Jesus and *(b)* in the aftermath or results of Jesus's resurrection, as the apostles and others serve as witnesses to the resurrection as the Spirit enables them (Acts 1:8; 2:1-13). As a whole, Luke-Acts comprises more than a fourth of the whole New Testament collection and is more than 15 percent longer than the entire Pauline corpus. The prominence and sheer size of Luke-Acts suggest that the distinctive Lukan perspective ought to find a greater place within New Testament theology and even Christian theology more generally (perhaps even out of the Pauline shadows!) than what has often been the case within the histories of Christian thought and biblical interpretation.

Authorship

Like the Gospel of Luke (and the other New Testament Gospels), the book of Acts is an anonymous text: the biblical text identifies no author. Most of what may be known about the author comes only from hints that the narrative discloses. Although persons often attempt to discover or defend the identification of the "real" or historical author with such textual evidence, the text itself only suggests what is commonly known as the "implied author." The implied author may be constructed from textual clues about that author's background, knowledge, point of view, and so on.

From Acts, readers are able to conclude that the author had superior literary skills in comparison to most other New Testament writers and was masterful in dramatic storytelling. The extensive use of the Septuagint (the Greek version of the Old Testament), both in allusions to stories and in vocabulary from the Torah, suggests the author was quite knowledgeable of the Jewish Scriptures. Although the common assumption is that this work came from the hand of a Gentile, this noticeable familiarity with the Scriptures indicates that he was either *(a)* a Gentile with a significant prior interest in and knowledge of the Jewish religion and practices or *(b)* a Diaspora/Hellenistic Jew. If the former instance describes the author, such knowledge of and exposure to the Jewish faith would have likely occurred through association with the synagogue as a Godfearer, a Gentile attracted to the worship, practices, and ethics of Judaism without "formal" conversion to the religion (see, e.g., Cornelius in Acts 10). If the author was Jewish by birth or conversion, as the second option describes, an apparent lack of knowledge about some aspects of Palestinian Judaism suggests someone who was not from the Palestinian region but from a different part of the Roman Empire (e.g., a traditional location for the writing of Acts is Antioch in Syria, which is northeast of that region).

The most prominent aspect of Acts that has been cited when addressing the question of authorship is the surprising appearance of first-person narration in some seemingly random sections of the last half of the book. Most of Acts, like other biblical narratives, is narrated from a third-person perspective (i.e., the narrator offers stories to readers about others). But in Acts 16, that perspective abruptly changes to first person without warning: "After Paul had seen the vision, *we* got ready at once to leave for Macedonia, concluding that God had called *us* to preach the gospel to them" (v. 10, NIV; emphases added). This first-person narration extends through verse 17, only to vanish from the story. It later reappears (20:5-15; 21:1-18; 27:1–28:16), only to disappear again. The earliest and traditional interpretation of this literary feature is that it indicates the author of Acts (and thus of the Gospel of Luke) was a ministry companion of the apostle Paul.

According to early church tradition from the late second century CE, Luke the physician and coworker of Paul wrote both the Gospel now attributed to him and the book of Acts. The early church father Irenaeus cites these "we" passages in Acts as evidence that the author of Acts was also one of Paul's ministry associates (*Against Heresies* 3.14.1; cf. 3.1.1; 3.13.3). This tradition is repeated by others, including Clement of Alexandria (*Miscellanies* 5.12), Tertullian (*Against Marcion* 4.2), and Origen (according to Eusebius, *Ecclesiastical History* 6.25). Even the important manuscript $\mathbf{P}^{75}$ (likely from the late second or third century CE) inserts the title "Gospel according to Luke" for the Third Gospel, thereby reflecting this tradition. But this information about Luke as the author of the Lukan Gospel and Acts depends on scarce New Testament references about this specific individual. Paul identifies him as a "fellow worker" (Philem. v. 24). Two other references identify him as "the beloved physician" (Col. 4:14, NRSVue) who still accompanied Paul as he was facing imminent death (2 Tim. 4:11). However, these references offer no actual support for Lukan authorship. Although the letters (whether or not from Paul's hand) may place Paul with

Luke from time to time, they do not definitely link them together during the specific "we" passages.

Differences in perspective, including differences between the depiction of Paul in Acts and Paul's self-depiction in the Pauline Letters, have led many Lukan interpreters to other conclusions, both about the first-person narration in Acts and about the authorship of the book. Some explain such shifts in narration to be the result of the author's reliance on a specific source for these parts of the work. But since other parts of the work indicate an author with advanced literary skills, it would seem unlikely that the same author who apparently was adept at editing other sources could not recognize and adapt such materials in these instances, even if other sources were consulted. Another possible solution is that the first-person perspective was inserted at strategic narrative points for rhetorical or literary effects to capture the reader's attention. Some downplay this possibility because the recipient of both Luke and Acts seems to have known the author (see the preface to each book: Luke 1:1-4; Acts 1:1-5); yet the effects of this type of literary device should not be underestimated.

The scarcity of information and evidence about the person identified as Luke in the New Testament and his authorship of Acts (and more broadly Luke-Acts) suggests that an interpreter should use caution when drawing conclusions about such matters, especially if such conclusions may influence how he or she reads and interprets these texts. A couple of considerations about authorship should be noted here. First, more "traditional" views of the authorship of Acts, including attempts to defend Luke the physician as the author of Acts (and the Gospel of Luke) by insisting that the narrator's style and perspective reveal tendencies of a person from the medical profession, often misinterpret aspects of the work itself.[3] An interpreter should be cautious of any theory of authorship that "imports" or forces ideas into the textual/narrative world of the work in

---

3. See, for example, Henry J. Cadbury, *The Style and Literary Method of Luke*, Harvard Theological Studies 6 (Cambridge, MA: Harvard University Press, 1920).

question. Second, the different explanations for the "we" passages in Acts suggest that a reader of Luke-Acts should not be quick to assume that this feature discloses authorial information. The divergences between Acts and the Pauline Letters raise questions about whether the pronoun "we" in Acts includes the author of Acts. These differences should cause an interpreter to reexamine whether the author accompanied or knew Paul or, at the very least, to consider the role of such differences within the book of Acts. However, for convenience most interpreters (including this one) still refer to the author of Luke-Acts as Luke, although the mystery of his identity remains. The anonymity of Acts implies that its interpretation does not depend on the resolution of authorship issues.[4]

> **The anonymity of Acts implies that its interpretation does not depend on the resolution of authorship issues.**

Addressee or Audience

The prefaces of the Gospel of Luke and the book of Acts both address these works to the same individual: Theophilus. The name literally means a "friend/ lover of God" or "beloved of God." Thus the focus can be on (1) the addressee's love of God, (2) God's love for that person, or (3) both. This individual is mentioned nowhere else in the New Testament or early Christian literature, even though the name itself is commonly attested in writings since the third century BCE. The honor with which Luke addresses Theophilus in the two prefaces (Luke 1:3; Acts 1:1) hints that he is a person of prominent social standing. A common view is that he was a wealthy patron who sponsored Luke's research and writing of these two volumes. Another popular view, because of

---

4. Thus, for purposes of this work, several different references will be used for the author of Acts, including "the Lukan author," "the Lukan narrator," and also "Luke." In the latter case, the name is a convenient label for the author or narrator of this work and should not imply an endorsement of the traditional view that Luke the physician was the author of Acts.

the meaning of Theophilus's name, is that this is a pseudonym, which either protected the actual recipient of the work or addressed all believers who are "beloved of God." Since the use of a name for symbolic reasons was uncommon in ancient literary practice, it is more likely that the original addressee was a specific believer (although other believers probably would have gathered together to hear the work read aloud to them).

Yet the materials of the work of Acts suggest that it was written not only for one individual but also for a more expanded audience characterized as those "beloved of God." Like authorship, the identity of this broader Lukan "implied audience" may be constructed from textual hints in Acts. Thus, like the author, the audience not only would have understood the Greek language (specifically Koine or common Greek) but also would have shared the author's knowledge of the Septuagint and its orientation for faith and life. This extensive familiarity with the Septuagint should challenge the common assumption that the implied audience (like the implied author) was completely pagan (and therefore Gentile) in background. At the very least, such an audience was probably much more diverse, both in background and origin. Given the issues that arise in Acts, it may have included both Jewish and Gentile believers, perhaps dealing with similar questions about diversity. The references to a variety of groups— Jews and Gentiles, men and women, wealthy and poor, citizens and slaves, prominent and marginal—suggest the possibility of a diverse social composition within this implied audience too.

Date of Composition

Three viable options exist for the date of composition of Acts. The oldest and traditional date is associated with the end of the book, which describes Paul's house arrest in Rome (in the early 60s CE). Some as early as Jerome (late fourth century to early fifth century CE) maintained that Acts (as well as the Gospel of Luke) was written during the short span between Paul's custody in Rome and his death a few years later. This dating of the Lukan corpus continues to have some contemporary advocates who typically offer three main reasons for their position. First, the abrupt ending to the book of Acts offers no information about Paul's release or subsequent death, which they interpret as a sign that the author wrote prior to Paul's tragic demise. Second, Luke mentions nothing about two important events: the persecution of Christians by the emperor Nero in 64 CE and the destruction of Jerusalem in 70 CE. Third, there is no mention in Acts of any of the Pauline Letters, which would have been collected and circulating among the earliest churches a few decades later. Despite the fact that such reasons may seem convincing at first glance, few Lukan scholars hold to this view today.

A more prominent view with Lukan and New Testament studies is that Luke-Acts was written as a two-volume work after the destruction of Jerusalem (70 CE), most likely in the 80s. Behind this view are passages in the Third Gospel where Jesus apparently alludes to the fate of Jerusalem (Luke 13:35; 19:43-44; 21:20-24; 23:28-31). Although such words could have been written prior to that catastrophic event, they would have had much greater significance after the city's destruction and demise. However, this position also underscores the significance of passages in Acts that refer to the closing of the temple gates in Jerusalem behind Paul after he was forcefully removed from the premises by an angry, violent mob (Acts 21:30). Like those passages citing Jesus's words about Jerusalem in the Lukan Gospel, this passage describing a distinctive act of hostility against one of the Christian movement's leaders would take on more significance after the subsequent breach between Judaism and the followers of Jesus. The later date proposed here also precedes the likely time when the Pauline collection of letters would have been gathered together and circulated, thereby explaining what many perceive to be a lack of knowledge about them as reflected in the Acts narrative. An advantage of this option for dating Acts (and the Gospel of Luke) is that it does not force historical explanations for the book's ending that may have better rhetorical or literary explanations.

A third theory for the date of composition is that Acts was written during the first half of the second century. The classic formulation of this view was offered by Ferdinand Christian Baur, a prominent New Testament scholar in the first half of the nineteenth century who contended that Acts played a pivotal role within early Christianity. According to Baur, the early church was comprised of two competing factions: the Jewish Christians (first led by Peter), who held to a strict observance of the Torah, and the Gentile Christians (first led by Paul), who considered the Torah to be ineffective. Baur interpreted Acts as a work seeking conciliation and concessions between both sides as the conflict continued into the second century.[5] Few contemporary scholars would accept Baur's view without substantial modification.

More recent proposals for a second-century dating of the composition of Acts consider other features of the work. One suggestion is that the vocabulary of Acts, its possible intertextual links (e.g., Josephus, whose last volume dates around 93 CE), and Luke's depiction of "the other" (such as the Jews)—all point to an early second-century date, perhaps 110-20 CE.[6] Another related view suggests that Acts may have been written as a response to the heretic Marcion.[7] The suggestion is that the author of Acts amended and edited a pre-Marcionite version of the canonized Gospel of Luke to serve as the first volume before Acts, or Acts's "prequel." In turn, Acts was written to "save" Paul from the distortions of false Marcionite teachings. This would date the composition of the Gospel of Luke and the book of Acts no earlier than the 140s and would correlate with Irenaeus's first references to both books.[8] Such later dates for the composition of Acts may also explain the existence of possible allusions

5. See Ferdinand Christian Baur, *Paul, the Apostle of Jesus Christ, His Life and Work, His Epistles and His Doctrine: A Contribution to a Critical History of Primitive Christianity*, 2 vols., trans. E. Zeller, ed. A. Menzies (London: Williams and Norgate, 1876), 1:1-145.

6. See Richard I. Pervo, *Dating Acts: Between the Evangelists and the Apologists* (Santa Rosa, CA: Polebridge, 2006).

7. See John Knox, *Marcion and the New Testament: An Essay in the Early History of the Canon* (Chicago: University of Chicago Press, 1942).

8. See Joseph B. Tyson, *Marcion and Luke-Acts: A Defining Struggle* (Columbia, SC: University of South Carolina Press, 2006), and Shelly Matthews, *Perfect Martyr: The Stoning of Stephen and the Construction of Christian Identity* (New York: Oxford University Press, 2010), 27-53.

to Pauline and deutero-Pauline letters in the Acts narrative. They also provide some rhetorical explanation for differences between the Lukan portrayal of Paul in Acts and the self-portrayal of Paul in the Pauline Letters.

Sources and Intertextual Issues

The specific questions about sources behind Luke-Acts focus on different issues because of what the two volumes themselves suggest about their sources. On the one hand, the preface of Luke's Gospel (Luke 1:1-4) explicitly describes the author's consultation of other sources, which various similarities shared with other Synoptic Gospels seem to confirm. For instance, the "two-source hypothesis"—a contemporary explanation for the so-called Synoptic problem, which identifies the similarities among the three Synoptic Gospels as well as shared (even verbatim) teachings of Jesus in the Matthean and Lukan Gospels that differ with the version found in Mark's Gospel—contends that Matthew and Luke appropriated two main sources for much of their respective Gospels: (1) Mark's Gospel and (2) a written source containing Jesus's teachings, known as "Q" after the German word for source, *Quelle*.

On the other hand, the book of Acts indicates nothing explicitly about sources behind the work. As mentioned earlier about the author, some contend that the passages that offer first-person narration (rather than the typical third-person perspective) in Acts reflect the perspective of a distinctive source that may have been written by a ministry companion of Paul or someone else who was present during those narrated times. However, other plausible explanations make that specific argument less than appealing. Yet there is little doubt that Luke had sources in hand for writing Acts. The problem lies in determining what those sources may have been and what they contained, since Luke the writer and storyteller was masterful in shaping the final text with his own style and vocabulary. One common view is that Luke had at least two sources: one that originated from Jerusalem and another from Antioch of Syria. The basic reason behind this proposal is the shift in action from the Holy City (Acts 1–7) to the latter as the narrative focus moves from the early church and Peter's ministry to Paul's ministry (Acts 13–21).

An important question about available sources for the book of Acts has to do with the Pauline Letters. Was the collection of these letters available to Luke as a source? It would seem as though the differences between Paul's letters and materials in Acts would be evidence against the availability of that collection for the author. It is also quite surprising that if such a collection was available, Luke never mentions Paul writing letters to the local churches within the narrative that he started. Yet as important as these issues are, one may also offer explanations other than Lukan unfamiliarity with the Pauline Letters. That is, there may be evidence of Lukan familiarity with specific Pauline Letters (e.g., Galatians, as seen perhaps in Acts 15 or 21, and Ephesians in Acts 20:17-38). One must be careful not to assume such familiarity a priori. But if such evidence emerges out of the careful study of the text of Acts, this would indicate the use of the Pauline Letters as a source. If Acts was written during the first half of the second century (see the previous section, "Date of Composition," p. 19), it is much more likely that the Pauline Letters as a collection was available to Luke as a source.

One additional source that was influential in the composition of Acts was the Septuagint. Luke borrows stylistic features and means of telling good stories from various sources. But he both makes use of the biblical mode of storytelling and echoes the Septuagint's vocabulary to shape and tell the narrative found in the Third Gospel and Acts.[9] These intertextual connections between the Septuagint and Acts may be seen in a couple of ways. First, Luke offers scriptural quotations (from the Septuagint) at strategic points within the Acts narrative. For instance, Peter's explanation of the Pentecost event includes a quotation

---

9. See Craig A. Evans and James A. Sanders, *Luke and Scripture: The Function of Sacred Tradition in Luke-Acts* (Minneapolis: Fortress, 1993), and Kenneth D. Litwak, *Echoes of Scripture in Luke-Acts: Telling the History of God's People Intertextually,* Journal for the Study of the New Testament: Supplemental Series 282 (New York: T. and T. Clark, 2005).

from the prophet Joel (see Acts 2:17-21). Also, early proclamations about Jesus as the Messiah include quotations from Psalm 16 (Acts 2:25-28), Deuteronomy 18 (Acts 3:22-23), and Psalm 118 (Acts 4:11). Second, Luke's storytelling and vocabulary often connect to themes and stories from Israel's Scriptures. There are scriptural echoes throughout Acts, as these materials draw on Israel's story to show that it continues among Jesus's followers and successors. In other words, the Lukan author appropriates these intertextual links to tell the ongoing story of God's purposes of salvation as told in Israel's Scriptures.

Textual-Critical Issues

Like other New Testament books, there are variations among Greek manuscripts of the text of Acts, although most are relatively minor. Such differences may be attributed either to copying texts by hand or to attempts at clarifying instances of textual ambiguity. However, notable differences exist within the Lukan corpus between two major textual traditions, commonly known as the Alexandrian and Western traditions. The Alexandrian tradition includes copies of both the Gospel of Luke and the book of Acts from as early as the fourth century, with the oldest papyrus copy of Luke's Gospel, $\mathbf{P}^{75}$, dating from 175 to 225 CE. The Western tradition includes parchment copies of both books from as early as the sixth century, as well as papyrus fragments and citations from early patristic writers (e.g., Tertullian, Cyprian, and Augustine) that date back to the third century.

The comparison of the texts of the Third Gospel and Acts from these two textual traditions reveals a major difference between them. The Western tradition omits or excludes materials from Luke 22–24 that are found in the Alexandrian tradition (Luke 22:19b-20; 24:3b, 6a, 12, 36b, 40, 51a, 52b), and yet the Western texts typically *expand* Acts when compared to the Alexandrian texts. These expanded Western materials of the Acts narrative amplify some stories, explain selected textual ambiguities, emphasize the apostles' authority, underscore Jewish rejection, and highlight the role of the Holy Spirit in a literary style that is notably different from the rest of the book. The result is an expanded version of the Western text of Acts that is about 10 percent longer than the Alexandrian one. Thus biblical translations of Acts are based on the Alexandrian version, due to the consistent editorial revision through the expansion of the text of Acts that the Western tradition reflects. Nonetheless, the Western text sometimes offers helpful clarification about some aspects of textual ambiguity, so interpreters should note textual variations when they exist.

Genre of Acts

Unstated assumptions and expectations accompany any conventional literary form or genre. Since different genres naturally function differently, their identification and assessment contribute significantly to the reading and interpretation of any text, including the book of Acts. Two general issues tend to complicate the precise identification of genre for Acts. One issue is the association of the Third Gospel with the book of Acts as a two-volume work. This raises the question about whether the unity of Luke-Acts requires "generic" unity.[10] On the one hand, one work might seem to necessitate one genre. On the other hand, the differences in subject and materials between the two books might make two genres more likely, however interpreters may understand the connections between them. Second, ancient literary conventions often obscured lines of delineation between different genres. Although such tendencies would not have made generic distinctions unimportant, shared characteristics among genres were the result. Since the study and imitation of different forms of literature were prominent means of learning composition within Greco-Roman education, readers should not be surprised to find such literary techniques and traits across generic lines. Such is the case in the book of Acts, with literary features

---

10. See Mikeal C. Parsons and Richard I. Pervo, *Rethinking the Unity of Luke and Acts* (Minneapolis: Fortress, 1993), 20-44.

of different genres found there. As a result, numerous proposals about the genre of Acts have been offered,[11] which may be grouped into two general categories.

One category identifies the genre of Acts (or Luke-Acts) as *biography*. The genre of biography is typically associated with the New Testament Gospels, with parallels noted between these works (each written as a "life of Jesus") and other Hellenistic biographies.[12] However, Luke-Acts has also been compared to works such as Diogenes Laertius's *Lives of Eminent Philosophers* (third century CE), which provides biographies of founders of religious movements or schools.[13] A significant feature of works such as Laertius's *Lives* is a dual focus on both the lives of those "founding fathers" and stories about the disciples or successors of those founders who followed in their footsteps. According to such proposals, this characteristic may be identified generally within Luke-Acts: the Gospel of Luke depicts the life of Jesus, and the book of Acts depicts stories of some of Jesus's leading successors (notably the apostles, especially Peter, in the first half, and Paul, in the second half). This understanding helps one in reading Luke-Acts more holistically. But the category of biography as a generic category is more convincing for the Gospel of Luke separately than it is either for Luke-Acts collectively or for the book of Acts separately.

A second category identifies the genre of Acts (or Luke-Acts) as *history* or *historiography*. Proposals regarding the book of Acts as some form of historiography often recognize the preface of the Third Gospel (Luke 1:1-4) and the opening of Acts (Acts 1:1) as consistent with prefaces that appear in Greco-Roman historiographies, either in basic form or in vocabulary and themes reflecting that tradition. For instance, Luke's description of his own inquiry and consultation of sources behind his work compares with what the Greek

---

11. See Thomas E. Phillips, "The Genre of Acts: Moving toward a Consensus?" *Currents in Biblical Research* 4, no. 3 (2006): 365-96.

12. See, e.g., Richard A. Burridge, *What Are the Gospels? A Comparison with Graeco-Roman Biography*, 2nd ed., The Biblical Resource Series (Grand Rapids: Eerdmans, 2004).

13. Charles H. Talbert, *Literary Patterns, Theological Themes, and the Genre of Luke-Acts*, Society of Biblical Literature Monograph Series 20 (Missoula, MT: Scholars, 1974).

historians Herodotus (*Histories* 1.1) and Thucydides (*History* 1.20.3; 1.22.2) stated about their own histories. Luke's specific depiction of his work as "accurate" (*akribōs*; Luke 1:3, AT) echoes how other historians described their work to their readers (e.g., Thucydides, *History* 1.22.2; Polybius, *Histories* 1.14.6; 16.20.8; 34.4.2; Dionysius of Halicarnassus, *Roman Antiquities* 1.1.2; 1.5.4; 1.6.3; and Josephus, *Jewish War* 1.2, 6, 9). Luke's portrayal of his work as an "orderly account" (Luke 1:3) corresponds with themes of other historiographical works, where historians underscore their own hands in the arrangement and unification of their respective works (see, e.g., Polybius, *Histories* 1.3.4; 1.4.2-3). Thus, in the case of Luke-Acts, Luke as both author and historian was responsible for connecting the stories of Jesus and the church to the story of Israel and to the broader story of human history. He does this by referring to events and persons from both the Old Testament and the Greco-Roman world.

There are several overlapping variations within the general category of historiography for the genre of Acts as interpreters attempt to deal with distinctive aspects of the work. Some view Acts as a popular form of *general history*, which focuses on the identity and rise of a particular people.[14] Others understand Acts to be a type of *historical monograph*, which is shorter than the typical historiographical work in part because it focuses on selected narrated events in a more confined time frame than do its longer historiographical counterparts.[15] Still others give more specific attention to the didactic or rhetorical purposes behind Acts, since discussions within Greco-Roman historiographical circles often raised concerns about such issues. Thus some have classified Acts as *apologetic history* because of its concerns to defend the Christian movement and

---

14. See David E. Aune, *The New Testament in Its Literary Environment*, Library of Early Christianity 8 (Philadelphia: Westminster, 1987), 77-157.

15. Eckhard Plümacher, "Die Apostelgeschichte als historische Monographie," in *Les Actes des Apôtres: Traditions, rédaction, théologie*, ed. J. Kremer, Bibliotheca ephemeridum theologicarum lovaniensium 48 (Leuven, BEL: Leuven University Press, 1979), 457-66; and Darryl W. Palmer, "Acts and the Ancient Historical Monograph," in *The Book of Acts in Its Ancient Literary Setting*, ed. B. W. Winter and A. D. Clarke, The Book of Acts in Its First Century Setting 1 (Grand Rapids: Eerdmans, 1993), 1-30.

its leaders from charges or accusations against them.[16] The Lukan tendency to draw parallels between biblical (notably Deuteronomistic and prophetic) traditions of the Septuagint and narrated events has led some to describe Acts as *biblical history*.[17] Yet the similarities between Acts and *political histories* of the Greco-Roman era, which connect founder, ancestors, and successors through a shared common story, suggest the possibility of some generic influence in this area as well.[18]

All these different variations of historiography attempt to address specific characteristics of the book of Acts. Yet there are also some aspects of the narrative that do not coincide with some of the more formal or technical characteristics of the Greco-Roman historiographical tradition. The prefaces of both the Gospel of Luke (Luke 1:1-4) and Acts (Acts 1:1-5) contain some vocabulary reflective of Greco-Roman historiographical emphases. However, rather than reflecting the literary style and conventions that conform to the standards of *formal* Greco-Roman historiography, these prefaces were composed in more accessible forms. These materials were more suitable for persons of the "professions" or trades.[19] Although these qualities would not detract from their historiographical nature, they would make these two works more comparable to other New Testament texts in their accessibility, even though they display greater literary style than most of their New Testament counterparts. This "popular" style of history writing would locate the book of Acts on the fringes of the historiographical genre rather than within the mainstream of that tradition. Nonetheless, Acts would still be recognized as history.

---

16. Gregory E. Sterling, *Historiography and Self-Definition: Josephus, Luke-Acts, and Apologetic Historiography* (Leiden, NL: Brill, 1992).

17. See, e.g., Brian S. Rosner, "Acts and Biblical History," in *The Book of Acts in Its Ancient Literary Setting*, ed. B. W. Winter and A. D. Clarke, The Book of Acts in Its First Century Setting 1 (Grand Rapids: Eerdmans, 1993), 65-82, and Thomas L. Brodie, "Luke-Acts as an Imitation and Emulation of the Elijah-Elisha Narrative," in *New Views on Luke and Acts*, ed. E. Richard (Collegeville, MN: Liturgical, 1990), 78-85.

18. See David L. Balch, "The Genre of Luke-Acts: Individual Biography, Adventure Novel, or Political History?" *Southwestern Journal of Theology* 33, no. 1 (Fall 1990): 5-19.

19. Loveday C. A. Alexander, *The Preface to Luke's Gospel: Literary Convention and Social Context in Luke 1.1–4 and Acts 1.1*, Society for New Testament Studies Monograph Series 78 (Cambridge, UK: Cambridge University Press, 1993).

The popular form of the book of Acts increases the likelihood that different features from different genres may have contributed to the work. Since literary education in the ancient world typically employed the stylistic imitation of classic writers, works such as Acts have been studied to assess such literary, creative, and compositional aspects alongside their historiographical qualities. Increased focus has been given to Luke's concerns for dramatic effect and good storytelling, both reflecting a desire to hold an audience's attention or interest.[20] But similarities between ancient epics and some episodes in Acts suggest these Lukan stories were told in familiar ways so that readers would *(a)* hear these latter accounts in light of those epochal events and *(b)* thus receive them in a way that accentuated their impact.[21] An author like Luke would have used such means of telling stories in more popular forms of history, such as the book of Acts (and the Third Gospel), in order to compose a work that would accomplish its purposes effectively (see Luke 1:1-4).

> **The popular form of the book of Acts increases the likelihood that different features from different genres may have contributed to the work.**

Questions for Consideration

1. What issues stand out for you as most significant within the interpretive process? How so?

2. What are some key arguments about the authorship of the Acts of the Apostles? What might be the importance of such considerations for interpreting this book or other books of the New Testament?

---

20. See Richard I. Pervo, *Profit with Delight: The Literary Genre of the Acts of the Apostles* (Philadelphia: Fortress, 1987).

21. Dennis R. MacDonald, "The Shipwrecks of Odysseus and Paul," *New Testament Studies* 45 (1999): 88–107; and Dennis R. MacDonald, "Paul's Farewell to the Ephesian Elders and Hector's Farewell to Andromache: A Strategic Imitation of Homer's *Iliad*," in *Contextualizing Acts: Lukan Narrative and Greco-Roman Discourse*, ed. T. Penner and C. V. Stichele (Atlanta: Society of Biblical Literature, 2003), 189-203.

3. What do you understand to be the major arguments behind contemporary trends that associate the Gospel of Luke and the Acts of the Apostles together as a two-volume work called "Luke-Acts"? How convinced are you that these two books are related or to be read together?

4. What are the different possibilities for the genre of the book of Acts? How does the consideration of genre influence how a biblical book such as Acts is read and interpreted?

2

Reading and Interpreting Acts as a Narrative

It is not surprising that most readers of the Bible approach biblical texts similarly. After all, these texts tend to have similar formats on the printed page or digital screen. And all the materials are divided into chapters and verses. Poetry is often (but not always) presented in a way that helps the reader recognize the unique material it is. But readers may be inclined to read letters and narratives similarly because of these resemblances in appearance "on the page."

Yet the book of Acts is a narrative text that brings with it different assumptions and expectations from those of other genres. Whereas letters tend to be much more direct and focus on the original recipients' specific situations, narratives are more indirect and call instead for readers to give their attention to the setting as depicted uniquely in that narrative. Unlike the *explicit* instructions, encouragement, or even commands that appear in letters, biblical narratives tend to be more *implicit* and seek to stimulate the *theological imagination* of readers so that they see things differently from the way they did before. Thus, although letters tend to tell their original recipients what might be expected of them, narratives are more open ended and leave their readers with more responsibility for conclusions and interpretation.[1]

---

1. The interpretation of a letter begins with a significant principle: that an instruction or command for a *specific* setting is not made to be universal. Rather, an interpreter first seeks to understand the theological issue at stake behind the instruction or command. However, the narrative encourages more interpretive possibilities.

31

Such differences are significant when considering matters such as the theology of Acts. Often, persons identify particular theological themes or threads from the book and suggest that these compose its theology. But such attempts too frequently fail to consider how these themes intersect with or relate to one another. As Beverly Gaventa correctly notes, such approaches treat Acts "as if it were a theological argument somehow encased—or even imprisoned—in a narrative. The assumption seems to be that Luke has a thesis or main point to demonstrate, and he creates his story in order to bear the thesis."[2] Rather than understanding the theology or "the point of the passage" as something to be extracted from the narrative, the interpreter must recognize such matters as deeply interwoven with the story Acts tells and inseparable from both that story and the reader's experience of engaging it.

> **The narrative of Acts tells a particular story in a particular way so that its readers *(a)* might see God at work among God's people in new ways and *(b)* might imagine what that might look like in their own settings.**

Such an understanding of how to read and interpret narratives like Acts (and the Gospels) recognizes the unique ways such materials are to function. The book of Acts does not offer a mere collection of historical records about what happened in the earliest decades of the Jesus movement (or the early church). Nor does it provide an idealized account about how Jesus's followers embodied Jesus's call to be his witnesses throughout the Mediterranean world (see Acts 1:8). But as a narrative, the function of this work is also not paradigmatic, since it does not provide some sort of theological blueprint or guidebook for the church or believers as a model that others (including contemporary congregations and persons) would or should later copy and imitate.[3] Rather,

---

2. Beverly Roberts Gaventa, "Toward a Theology of Acts: Reading and Rereading," *Interpretation* 42, no. 2 (April 1988): 149-50.

3. See Eric D. Barreto, "A Gospel on the Move: Practice, Proclamation, and Place in Luke-Acts," *Interpretation* 72, no. 2 (April 2018): 175-76.

the narrative of Acts tells a particular story in a particular way so that its readers (a) might see God at work among God's people in new ways and (b) might imagine what that might look like in their own settings. As Luke Timothy Johnson states, "The first readers of Luke's narrative would perhaps not have seen his story as a nostalgic recollection of a time past but rather as a summons to an ideal that might be in danger of being lost, not as a work of blank historiography but as a thrilling act of utopian imagination, less a neutral report on how things were than as a normative prescription for how things ought to be."[4]

So how might readers of Acts go about engaging this book in such ways? Such "imaginative" reading does not ignore the textual details of the Acts narrative. But such readings of Acts must also give careful attention to the narrative features of Acts. Several narrative features stand out as significant for any reading of the book of Acts.

The Two Levels of Narrative

A narrative approach to a biblical book such as Acts (or narrative criticism) considers the literary or storied quality of that work. The focus is on the final form of the biblical text before the reader and not on possible issues that may have contributed to the text's production (e.g., source or redaction criticism). The interpreter's attention is on key storied elements that contribute both to the narrative itself and to its reading from start to finish.

Narrative approaches to Acts often distinguish between two levels of narrative: story and discourse.[5] On the one hand, the *story level* of a narrative consists of the basic elements of what most readers would easily recognize in a narrative: the settings, the events, the characters, and so on. These may be described as the "what" of a story. On the other hand, the *discourse level* of a narrative consists

---

4. Luke Timothy Johnson, *Prophetic Jesus, Prophetic Church: The Challenge of Luke-Acts to Contemporary Christians* (Grand Rapids: Eerdmans, 2011), 5.

5. This distinction was first proposed by Seymour B. Chatman, *Story and Discourse: Narrative Structure in Fiction and Film* (Ithaca, NY: Cornell University Press, 1978).

of the various ways that the author (or narrator) shaped those story elements to communicate and convey the narrative in its final form. Such elements are connected to the author's purposes in relation to the narrative. That is, the discourse level may be described as the "how" of a story. Thus, for instance, in Acts the appearance of the apostle Peter as a character in chapter 1 is part of the *story level* of the narrative. However, how the narrator depicts Peter as a reliable character is part of the *discourse level* of Acts.

Although the text itself does not distinguish between these two levels, the usefulness of this method lies in its ability to highlight *how* the story is told. This enables readers to recognize how the text could have been written differently and what perspective may shape the account as it stands.

The Elements of Narrative

The discourse level of a narrative is presumably where readers will find the more creative aspect of the author's narrative work, for this level offers the most direct evidence of the author's shaping of the work. Thus, although one cannot capture the author's intention at the time of writing, interpreters can consider what the text itself suggests about the author's purposes, since the discourse level (i.e., *how* the story is told) offers a window into such matters.

But what are some elements of narrative that would reflect such matters in the story of Acts? Several elements are considered here: (1) plot and selection, (2) characters, (3) repetition, and (4) assessments and commentary.

1. Plot and Selection

It may seem almost unnecessary to consider the development or crafting of plot for a narrative. After all, plot seems almost synonymous with narrative! Yet for a work like Acts, even Aristotle contended that plot would not arise merely out of a chronology of events or actions.[6] That is, someone was always

---

6. See Aristotle, *Poetics* 9.3; 23.2. See also Dionysius of Halicarnassus, *On Thucydides* 9 and *Letter to Gnaeus Pompeius* 3.

responsible for the order and arrangement of a narrative work, even histori-cal ones, and chronology was not the main contributor to it. The expectation was that an author of a work like Acts would give careful consideration to the arrangement and progression of the narrative. Thus an author would select and sequence episodes and events with such matters in mind, and this would ultimately contribute to the broader purposes and effects of the work itself.[7]

The significance of such plotting activities in Acts cannot be underestimat-ed. Such evidence may be found in various ways. For instance, at a broad level there is correspondence between the Lukan depiction of *(a)* the ministry of Jesus in Luke's Gospel and *(b)* the ministries of both Peter and Paul in Acts. The similarities between Jesus's journey from Galilee to Jerusalem in Luke's Gospel and Paul's ministry journeys in Acts also suggest that the author sought to describe Paul's activities as akin to those of Jesus. But interpreters should also explore how the Lukan author selected, arranged, and sequenced other materi-als in light of the purposes of Acts.[8]

2. Characters

Although narrative characters are considered later in this book, it is impor-tant to note here that characters are critical to a narrative because they typically bring the story to life. Readers may relate to some characters and even dislike others without recognizing the reasons for their responses. Yet even though ancient narratives tend not to offer fully developed characters, they still enter into the practice of characterization or of describing those characters in some ways and not others.

The tendency in an ancient narrative like Acts is to describe characters through indirect means. That is, readers learn what they do about a character largely through that character's own actions and speech, through what other

---

7. Richard P. Thompson, *Keeping the Church in Its Place: The Church as Narrative Character in Acts* (New York: T. and T. Clark, 2006), 12.

8. See how Jeannine K. Brown discusses plot in her work *The Gospels as Stories: A Narrative Approach to Matthew, Mark, Luke, and John* (Grand Rapids: Baker Academic, 2020), 23-42.

characters do or say in relation to that character, or in subtle comparison with other aspects of the narrative itself (whether positive or not). On occasion, the narrator may move beyond merely *showing* characters to readers to instead *telling* them something specific about a character (motivations, thoughts or emotions, vocation, gender, social status, appearance, etc.). Because characters interact with others, they tend to "play off" one another. Such interaction often reveals purposes behind the narrative.[9]

3. Repetition

One should not be surprised that repeated actions and themes are suggestive of emphases within Acts. Just as the author is responsible for selecting episodes and materials to include within the narrative, the author also decides what should be highlighted and how best that should happen. Such repetition may occur by reiterating an important scene (e.g., the Cornelius event or Saul's conversion). But that may also happen by using common images to depict characters similarly, either positively or negatively. This element of narrative is more indirect in nature, but its cumulative effect tends to make its point as a reader progresses through the narrative.

4. Assessments and Commentary

Although narratives rely more on readers to make judgments and conclusions about what they encounter in the story, narrators typically do not leave them to fend for themselves. Narrators use both indirect and direct means to guide the readers of their stories, even though those readers must still connect the dots themselves.

Generally speaking, ancient narratives like Acts are best known for the indirect means by which narrators or authors guide their readers. Thus specific materials of assessment or commentary that the narrator inserted into the narrative stand out for the careful reader. When the narrator offers a direct

---

9. See Thompson, *Keeping the Church*, 17-28, and Brown, *Gospels as Stories*, 65-83.

assessment of a situation or character (perhaps with a summary statement), such a comment is beneficial because it provides insightful information to assist readers as they interpret either what has happened or what will happen in the narrative. When the narrator offers indirect commentary of a situation through a reliable character, those remarks not only assist the reader's interpretation of the events in the narrative but also address readers more broadly.

The Perspective and Purpose of Narrative

Every narrative comes from a unique angle or perspective. Each seeks to offer us a glimpse into a world that we might not otherwise see. As Eric Barreto suggests,

> Narrative is imagination, a way of seeing the world differently, a story that will hit us in an unexpected way not because it tells us precisely what to do but because it gives us new perspective. Narrative shows us a world full of the beautiful and the grotesque, the sublime and the mundane. Narrative is about giving us a God-tinged imagination that sees God's face etched in the darkest corners of the world.[10]

But that also means we must read and engage Acts in ways that consider not only practices *for others* but also practices that open us up *to others*.[11] Reading must become more than a new set of words about an old set of words. Instead, such reading must result in the embodiment of what has been imaginatively encountered within the narrative of Acts.

The Limits of Narrative

One final consideration on the reading of the Acts narrative has to do with its "co-texts." Since all narratives construct what is known as a "narrative

---

10. Barreto, "Gospel on the Move," 185-86.
11. See, e.g., ibid., 182: "Too often in Christian communities, hospitality is limited to how we welcome others. That is, in too many churches, hospitality is something we offer others, not something we are willing to receive. In many churches, hospitality tends to be a practice more than an identity, a way of life. Jesus's hospitality upends expectations, making hosts of guests and guests of hosts."

world," a reader should consider the place of other biblical texts in relation to Acts. In other words, what other texts should a reader include within the narrative world of the book of Acts?

First, the book of Acts assumes a working knowledge of the Septuagint, the Greek translation of the Old Testament. So it is reasonable to expect the Old Testament (in general) to be foundational to the story depicted in Acts.

Second, the book of Acts assumes a familiarity with the life and teachings of Jesus as found in the Gospel of Luke. The common recipient (Theophilus) for both the Third Gospel and Acts and the overlap of material between the Gospel's ending (Luke 24) and the beginning of Acts suggest that *this* Gospel, *not the other three*, belongs within the narrative world of Acts (or Luke-Acts). Thus, when reading and interpreting Acts, a reader should refer *only to the Third Gospel as its co-text* when linking that narrative to the story of Jesus, not to other Gospel accounts.

We must read and engage Acts in ways that consider not only practices *for others* but also practices that open us up *to others.*

Third, despite the common interests between Acts and the New Testament letters (due to the inclusion of most letter authors as characters within the Acts narrative), the purposes of the respective authors require careful readers *initially* to interpret these materials separately to ensure that they hear and understand all these biblical voices. Turning too quickly to New Testament letters as co-texts (read with Acts) tends to squelch the perspective and purpose(s) of the Acts narrative.

Questions for Consideration

1. What does it mean for the book of Acts to be taken seriously as a narrative? How is that similar to or different from the ways that you have approached Acts in the past?

2. How does a narrative approach to reading Acts help us as readers to understand and listen to its purposes?

3. What do you think are (or might be) useful elements or features of the Acts narrative for revealing its message and purposes?

4. What are some possible connections between Acts and other parts of the Bible? How important do you see the relationship between the Gospel of Luke and the book of Acts?

PART II

READING AND INTERPRETING SELECTED TEXTS FROM ACTS

A. Speeches in Acts: Introduction

One of the prominent features of Acts that has attracted considerable scholarly attention is the Lukan use of speeches throughout the narrative (see, e.g., Acts 2, 3, 7, 13, 15, 17, and 20). Although these speeches appear on the lips of different characters, they often reflect similar themes consistent with what the narrative itself presents. In other words, most scholars argue that we see the narrator's hand in the presentation of these speeches. But since the narrator ultimately is the one who includes the material that finds its way into the narrative and excludes those things that do not, it is very appropriate to consider why someone would include so many lengthy speeches in the narrative. However, a more useful issue for consideration might be the function of these speeches within the book of Acts.

But the prominence of speeches in a literary work is not unique to the book of Acts. In the fifth century BCE, the ancient historian Thucydides explained his use of speeches in his history of the Peloponnesian War (*History* 1.22). As part of the so-called Greco-Roman historiographical tradition, Thucydides's understanding of the function of a speech in a historical narrative cast a long shadow of influence over the broader world of ancient narratives, even beyond the circles of historical writing. And Thucydides seems to have influenced the composition of the Gospel of Luke and the book of Acts, given the emphases in the preface of the Third Gospel (1:1-4) that mirror those of that tradition. In particular, a speech within a narrative did not serve *primarily* as a record of what happened but as implicitly explanatory or interpretive material. In other words, a speech functioned within its broader literary work to offer its reader materials that would help the reader understand or interpret what *had* happened in the narrative, what *was going* to happen in that narrative, or *both*.

One might wonder why these narrators did not simply address their audiences or readers directly and tell them explicitly what they needed to know. The narrator *could* (and sometimes did) offer such direct instructions or "explicit commentary" about the narrative action. Such guidance could ensure that readers interpreted the story as the narrators hoped. However, in the ancient world readers and audiences could become suspicious if they thought the narrators were attempting to control them and manipulate their conclusions.

So narrators tended to remain outside the view of their readers or audiences. They had other, more subtle, ways for guiding and assisting their readers and audiences. Speeches became common tools for narrators because they could use the speeches and conversations of characters within the narrative or story to provide what literary critics have called "implicit commentary." In an ancient narrative, such commentary would appear on the lips of narrative characters, usually reliable ones, to articulate particular interpretations or views that the narrative would espouse. Such perspectives would function within the broader narrative work by offering interpretive clues for readers as they proceeded through that work.

> **Reading and interpreting speeches in Acts will require attention to how the speeches function in relation to material before and after them and to their contributions to understanding the entire book.**

If one of the literary conventions used by the author of Acts was this distinctive use of speeches, then it is possible to see the potential roles of such speeches in the Acts narrative. Reading and interpreting speeches in Acts will require more of the reader than merely paying attention to the "internal" content of the speeches themselves. Rather, reading and interpreting speeches in Acts will require attention to how the speeches function in relation to material before and after them and to their contributions to understanding the entire book.

3

What Got into *Him?* Peter's Pentecost Speech

(ACTS 2:14-36)

There is little doubt that the Pentecost event, as recorded in Acts 2, functions as *the* prominent event in the entire Acts narrative. We see such prominence both in its placement at the beginning of Acts and in repeated allusions and references to it throughout the pages of Acts (e.g., in chs. 10, 11, 15, and 19). However, what is particularly noteworthy is that nowhere else in the writings of the New Testament do we find this extraordinary event mentioned. Although Pentecost stands prominently in Acts as the *single* event that both defines and clarifies everything else in the narrative, Pentecost as a notable event within the story of God occupies no place in the reflection and thought of the rest of the New Testament.

What is also remarkable about the Lukan rendition of Pentecost is that the author provides only a brief description of the actual event itself. That is, what happened on that infamous day among the earliest believers takes up a mere four verses (Acts 2:1-4)! Now one may rightly note that another nine verses (vv. 5-13) give attention to what onlookers thought about the unusual things that happened. Yet still, these subsequent verses describe the reactions of these onlookers, not the extraordinary things that occurred. And afterward, the narrative presents Peter's speech to the onlookers—a section that takes up more than twenty verses (vv. 14-36). If Pentecost is such a prominent event in the book of Acts, why does the narrator provide such little space to describe the spectacular event itself but then devote so much more attention to Peter's speech?

The prominence of speeches in ancient narratives like Acts suggests that Peter's speech does not appear here in Acts 2 simply because that is what happened. That is, Peter's speech functions as an explanation not only for the Jewish bystanders in Jerusalem but perhaps *more importantly* for the Lukan readers. Given the placement of this event and speech within the broader Acts narrative, attempts to read and interpret this speech must also consider its function in shaping the perspective of those readers as they peruse these Lukan stories (from Jesus's last days with the apostles in Acts 1 to Paul's unstoppable ministry in Rome in Acts 28). Thus one must consider *(a)* the major emphases of Peter's Pentecost speech and *(b)* the significant connections between this speech and later themes in Acts.

Peter's Explanatory Speech at Pentecost (Acts 2:14-36)

The extraordinary scene of the Spirit coming upon the believers and of the crowd of Jewish pilgrims hearing the gospel message in their native languages (Acts 2:4, 6) left a lot of confounded bystanders with unanswered questions that they voiced to one another (see vv. 12-13). Readers would have been equally confused. Peter's speech offers explanations for both groups. Several emphases emerge from the speech.

1. The Fulfillment of God's Promises and Purposes for Israel as the People of God

The citation of the Joel passage (Acts 2:17-21), which was a promise to Israel, explains from the Hebrew Scriptures that the phenomenon of the coming of the Spirit upon Jesus's followers evidenced God's fulfillment of that promise, which was to be part of God's eschatological acts of salvation on their behalf. The speech draws attention *away from* the extraordinary nature of the

Pentecost event and *toward* a simple fact: God acted as God promised long ago.

Although persons often declare that the Pentecost event signifies the birth of the church, the Lukan perspective through Peter's speech points instead to what God had done on behalf of *all Israel* as the people of God. That is, the Lukan ecclesiology, if you will, has a broader perspective from the outset, based on the Septuagint's use of the Greek term *ekklēsia* (translated "church" in the New Testament). What we find here was entirely a *Jewish* event that occurred during a *Jewish* festival, at the *Jewish* temple, with all-*Jewish* participants and bystanders, with the God of the *Jewish* people initiating what happened and implementing what *this* God had vowed centuries before. Its significance is in what God had done to fulfill God's promises and purposes among the people whom God had called.

Other appearances of the Spirit in the narrative, notably the instance at the house of Cornelius (10:44-46) and with the twelve men in Ephesus (19:1-7), allude back to this same Pentecost scene. However, other images of persons filled by the Spirit or receiving messages from the Spirit convey such individuals as God's prophets and reveal God at work.[1] The quotation from Joel underscores the Spirit's transcendence over traditional barriers of that era, so that all persons—female or male, young or old, enslaved or free—could serve as God's prophetic instruments (Acts 2:17-18).

2. The Role of God in the Resurrection of Jesus

Closely related to the divine fulfillment of God's promises and purposes for Israel is the role of God in the crucifixion and death of Jesus. Although Peter's speech makes it clear that the Jewish response to Jesus was the rejection of God's purposes, Peter also underscores several times that God responded first by undoing their murder of Jesus through his resurrection (see Acts 2:23-24, 33) and then by honoring Jesus through his ascension: God exalted Jesus by

---

1. See William H. Shepherd Jr., *The Narrative Function of the Holy Spirit as a Character in Luke-Acts*, Society of Biblical Literature Dissertation Series 147 (Atlanta: Scholars, 1994), esp. 245-50.

placing him in the position of divine honor and authority (vv. 33, 36). In other words, human rejection did not have the final word, God did (as always!). The speech does not offer specific explanation about the saving importance of Jesus's death and resurrection (e.g., through theories of atonement), although the later reference to repentance, baptism, and the forgiveness of sins (v. 38) is obviously linked to these.[2] Nonetheless, the Lukan focus on God's role in the reversal of what God's chosen people had done through their rejection of Jesus affirms the constancy and reliability of God's plans and purposes.

3. The Christological "Twist" to This Divine Fulfillment

A third theological emphasis that may be the core affirmation of this explanatory speech is the role of Jesus in God's fulfillment of the divine promises and purposes for Israel. The Lukan narrator depicts the Pentecost event in Jewish terms, and the citation of the Joel passage at the beginning of Peter's speech maintains a similar orientation. However, the repeated accent placed on the resurrected and exalted Jesus coaxes readers to see this divine fulfillment as a matter of *Christology* rather than view it as a matter of *pneumatology*, even though the narrative itself often uses Spirit language to describe the believers.[3]

In other words, the speech demands a radical change in perspective. Not only had God accomplished what God had promised, but also the agent who accomplished these divine promises and purposes among the Jewish people was none other than Jesus, the same one whom they were responsible for murdering. The crucial role of Jesus in this divine fulfillment is the distinctive aspect of Peter's message and the gospel as it was later proclaimed. The gospel message declared to God's people how God kept and accomplished those promises

---

2. Cf. H. Douglas Buckwalter, "The Divine Saviour," in *Witness to the Gospel: The Theology of Acts*, ed. I. H. Marshall and D. Peterson (Grand Rapids: Eerdmans, 1998), 107-20.

3. See Max Turner, "The 'Spirit of Prophecy' as the Power of Israel's Restoration and Witness," in *Witness to the Gospel*, 332-33.

to them: through Jesus as Lord and Christ (Acts 2:36).[4] That is, God raised and exalted Jesus as Lord and Christ, thereby giving the promised Spirit to Jesus (v. 33). Thus Jesus actually received the Spirit and was therefore the agent who "poured out" the Spirit. Without this distinctively *christological* emphasis concerning Pentecost, there would be little if anything about this event that would be distinctly related to the Christian gospel. Thus the Pentecost experience of the Jesus movement did not signify divine actions *apart* from the Jewish people but *within* them.[5] The outpouring of the Spirit through Jesus as Lord and Christ signifies how God fulfilled God's purposes and promises within God's own people.

> **The speech demands a radical change in perspective. Not only had God accomplished what God had promised, but also the agent who accomplished these divine promises and purposes among the Jewish people was none other than Jesus, the same one whom they were responsible for murdering.**

But this is where the common Lukan description of members of this movement as "believers" and the importance of "believing" or "faith" come into the picture. In most instances in Acts, believing is left undefined. However, in a few cases believing is qualified: "in the Lord" (Acts 9:42), "in him [Jesus]" (10:43), or "on the Lord Jesus" (16:31, AT). Or faith is clarified as being "in our Lord Jesus" (20:21) or "in me [Jesus]" (26:18). Interestingly, every qualification comes later after the initial period of the Jesus movement in Jerusalem. However, there is little mention of such faith after Acts 21 (except for 22:19; 24:24; 26:18). Here, it is enough to describe persons simply as "believing," because to believe is to embrace what God had done in Christ.

---

4. See C. Kavin Rowe, "Acts 2.36 and the Continuity of Lukan Christology," *New Testament Studies* 53, no. 1 (2007): 37-56.

5. See David Seccombe, "The New People of God," in *Witness to the Gospel*, 353-54, who refers to Luke's depiction of the church as a messianic people.

4. The Inclusive Dimension of That Salvific Promise

The last portion of the Joel passage, quoted in Acts 2:21, is widely recognized as programmatic for Acts as a whole: "And everyone who calls on the name of the Lord will be saved." In this Pentecost context, there is little doubt of a double meaning to this, since Peter says more than he knows. On the one hand, his later consternation over the vision with the unclean animals in Caesarea (10:9-19) indicates that he only could have understood this as a reference to the people of Israel. Similarly, the idea of including those beyond the people of Israel ("everyone," in 2:21) was not embraced by the church in Jerusalem, since the spread of the Christian movement outside of Jerusalem did not occur as an intentional response to Jesus's call (1:8) but as a result of the opposition after Stephen's death (8:1-3).

On the other hand, the broader context of Acts indicates that the saving implications of this promise extended far beyond the circles of the Jewish people and was inclusive of others as well. This inclusive aspect of the Christian message continually echoes throughout Acts in its use of "salvation" terms (notably *sōzō* and *sōtēria*), especially in Peter's two explanations about what happened with Cornelius (11:14; 15:11). Evidence of the concept is apparent wherever there are both Jewish and Gentile responses to the Christian message, whether the text explicitly mentions this or not. Yet tensions in Jewish synagogues over the Christian gospel message may have been indicative of the difficulties that came with receiving news of God's inclusive grace that opened doors of salvation and fellowship to those who had been deemed outsiders in the past (see, e.g., 13:42-52; 17:5-9, 10-13; 18:5-11).

Relation of Themes to the Broader Context of Acts

As the first major speech in Acts, Peter's explanatory speech at Pentecost provides the theological trajectories for the narrative holistically and, more specifically, for the ecclesiology of Acts. The pivotal points of Acts 10–11 and Acts

15 narrate and then twice interpret the Cornelius event in light of Pentecost and its explanatory speech. These pivotal points further indicate the importance of the theological and christological connections between the Pentecost scene and the rest of the book of Acts, which the Lukan narrator points out through Peter.

Interestingly, some of these themes and connections are readily seen at the end of the ministry portion of this narrative in another speech: the speech of Paul to the Ephesian elders at Miletus (20:17-36). This latter speech provides the opposite or latter bookend of the portion of Acts concerning the Lukan image or depiction of the church. Yet important emphases from Peter's Pentecost speech are reiterated in this later speech that Paul delivered in Miletus. For instance, Peter emphasized that God had fulfilled God's promise to Israel as the people of God—a promise first articulated by the prophet Joel (Acts 2:17-21). Similarly, Paul reiterated the divine initiative behind what the people had witnessed, since God was responsible for bringing the church into existence (20:28).[6] In Peter's speech, the emphasis is on Jesus as both Lord and Christ (2:36), who was God's agent in restoring Israel and calling the people to repent (v. 38). In Paul's speech, he, too, refers to the distinctive role of Jesus by speaking about repentance and "faith in our Lord Jesus" (20:21). Peter's speech reminded his audience inclusively that "everyone who calls on the name of the Lord will be saved" (2:21). Paul's speech reminded the Ephesians that he declared the gospel to everyone, including both Jews and Greeks (20:21).

In addition, between these two speeches in Acts are repeated references to the Christian message[7]—including instances where that message identifies

---

6. Cf. Beverly Roberts Gaventa, "Theology and Ecclesiology in the Miletus Speech: Reflections on Content and Context," *New Testament Studies* 50, no. 1 (January 2004): 48-49.

7. See, e.g., variations of the Greek term *logos* (or "word"; Acts 2:40; 4:4; 6:4; 8:4; 10:36, 44; 11:19; 13:26; 14:25; 15:7; 16:6; 17:11; 18:5; 20:32) for the gospel message, including *ho logos tou theou* ("the word of God"; 4:31; 6:2, 7; 8:14; 11:1; 12:24; 13:5, 7, 46; 17:13; 18:11) and *ho logos tou kyriou* ("the word of the Lord"; 8:25; 13:44, 49; 15:35-36; 16:32; 19:10, 20).

Jesus as Messiah[8]—that allude back to the inclusive emphases of the Pentecost speech (as well as the supplemental christological materials in the speeches of Acts 3 and 4). By framing the ministry of the earliest church with speeches affirming God's activity among God's people, the Lukan narrator assists his readers in how they should perceive God's work, despite the differences among the people themselves.

What is so surprising is that this Pentecost speech came from someone like Peter. Only several weeks earlier, he failed miserably to discern what was happening with Jesus. As a result, Peter wilted under the intense interrogation of a single servant girl and later two others who recognized him as one of Jesus's followers (see Luke 22:54-62). Now from Peter's lips come profound, prophetic words—a message that reveals what God was doing when no one else could recognize it! What got into *him*? Or maybe the message also answers the question: with the promised gift of God's Spirit comes the recognition of what God is up to and what God might do next. This speech is not merely a report about what happened but a clue to readers of Acts about what to look for—most notably in Acts and also among us as faithful readers of Scripture.

Questions for Consideration

1. What are some distinctive characteristics of speeches that may be relevant in the reading and interpreting of Acts?

2. How would you explain the Lukan author's decision to give more space in Acts to Peter's speech than to a description of what happened on the day of Pentecost?

---

8. See esp. Acts 8:5, 12; 9:22; 10:36, 48; 11:17; 17:3; 18:5, 28; 28:31. Note the significance of the theological themes, especially the inclusive aspect of salvation that would be associated with this christological message as the Jesus movement spread geographically.

3. What do you consider to be significant themes or emphases in Peter's Pentecost speech? How might the importance of these be similar or different for Peter's audience and the readers of Acts?

4. How do you see this speech related to the remainder of the book of Acts?

4

An Unappreciated/Explosive Speech:
Stephen's Jerusalem Speech
(ACTS 7:2-53)

Speeches appear throughout the book of Acts.[1] Some speeches are quite short;[2] others (like Peter's Pentecost speech in Acts 2 or Paul's speech in Pisidian Antioch in Acts 13) exceed four hundred words (in the Greek text). Many of these speeches stand out as prominent portions of the narrative by contributing significantly to the unfolding story of Acts. Often these speeches are interpreted merely as part of what happened within the earliest decades of the early church.

Among the speeches in Acts that are often ignored or avoided within the contemporary church is Stephen's speech before the Jewish council (7:2-53). Lectionary selections tend to gloss over or even overlook this speech, and many Bible study groups avoid the extended oration in favor of "action" texts. There is even a long-standing "belief" that Luke's account of Stephen's hearing before the Jewish council would have been more effective if the speech were omitted altogether, contending that the narrative account flows more smoothly by moving from 6:8-15 to 7:55–8:1.[3]

---

1. According to Marion Soards and his study of speeches in Acts, thirty-six speeches appear in Acts. See Marion L. Soards, *The Speeches in Acts: Their Content, Context, and Concerns* (Louisville, KY: Westminster/John Knox, 1994).

2. E.g., Gallio's speech to the Corinthian Jews (Acts 18:14b-15), Agabus's speech in Caesarea (21:11b-c), and Paul's speech to the disciples in Caesarea (21:13b-c).

3. See the comment of prominent Acts scholar F. J. Foakes-Jackson in "Stephen's Speech in Acts," *Journal of Biblical Literature* 49, no. 3 (1930): 284.

For many readers of Acts, the ordeal of Stephen—his so-called trial before the Jewish council and subsequent murder—stands out as a major turning point in the earliest days of the early church, since the persecution against the believers scattered most of them from Jerusalem to surrounding areas (see 8:1*b*-3). But these same readers remember or know little, if anything, about what Stephen may have said before that council and what ultimately may have provoked the murderous rage that led to his death.

Despite the lack of familiarity with what Stephen may have said, both the insertion and length of his speech—the longest among the speeches in Acts[4]— suggest that the Lukan author considered that speech important for readers of this narrative. This is especially so when considering the strategic role of Stephen's arrest and murder both for the earliest believers and for the unfolding story of Acts. Because of all that is associated with the broader situation involving Stephen in Acts 6–8, it is reasonable for interpreters of Acts to expect this speech to provide theological clues to make sense of such things.

The Context of the Speech (Acts 6:8-15)

The Lukan narrator offers little explanation for the disputes that arose between Stephen and "members of the Synagogue of the Freedmen" (Acts 6:9), who were likely Diaspora (and therefore Greek-speaking) Jews, as Stephen was.[5]

But such opposition resisted Stephen because he had done "great wonders and signs" (v. 8) among the Jewish people, a description that places him in the company of Jesus (2:22) and the apostles (v. 43; 5:12*a*; see 4:30). By using the same word to describe both Stephen's and the apostles' proclamation of the gospel (the Greek verb *laleō*; see 2:4, 6-7, 11; 4:1, 17, 20, 29; 5:20, 40), the

---

4. Stephen's speech is more than twice as long (over one thousand words in the Greek text) as any other speech in Acts. In the New Testament, only Jesus delivers a longer speech than this one.

5. The word "diaspora" derives from a Greek verb meaning "scatter." After the Babylonian Exile, most Jewish captives did not return to Israel. In later centuries, a large percentage of the Jewish populace scattered throughout the Mediterranean world. Such persons were more accustomed to navigating the issues associated with living out their Jewish heritage within a (Gentile) world and culture shaped by different perspectives and values.

narrator depicts the opposition against Stephen as similar to what the apostles faced earlier in Acts 4 and 5. However, in this instance the opponents relied on underhanded tactics by producing false witnesses to testify against Stephen before the Jewish council. The false witnesses accused him of speaking relentlessly "against this holy place and against the law," based on the teachings of Jesus (6:13; see vv. 13-14).

Two aspects of this so-called trial setting stand out. First, Stephen was left alone to face these charges. Thus, in addition to the apparent illegitimacy of the charges themselves, the scene itself is colored with tension and suspense, since it is reminiscent of what Jesus himself faced (alone) before the same council (Luke 22:66-71), a hearing that did not end favorably for Jesus. Second, the spectacular description of Stephen's countenance ("his face was like the face of an angel" [Acts 6:15]) is suggestive of either Moses's shining face (Exod. 34:29-35) or of Jesus's illumined presence at his transfiguration (Luke 9:29).[6] Either comparison depicts Stephen as reflecting God's glory and divine character. Such associations prepare not only the members of the Jewish council but also readers of Acts to encounter Stephen's speech as a message from God.

The Content of Stephen's Speech (Acts 7:2-53)

Since Stephen responded to the high priest's question, "Are these accusations true?" (Acts 7:1, CEB), one would expect the speech to deal directly with those issues as some sort of defense against the charges. Surprisingly, Stephen never addresses the charges directly. Instead, the speech offers "a summary of the patriarchal history with which every one of his auditors was thoroughly familiar."[7] However, Stephen's narrated story of Israel's history is very selective, focusing largely on two things: what God had done and how Israel's ancestors responded to God. In order to interpret this speech appropriately, a reader must

---

6. Richard P. Thompson, *Acts: A Commentary in the Wesleyan Tradition*, New Beacon Bible Commentary (Kansas City: Beacon Hill Press of Kansas City, 2015), 156.

7. Foakes-Jackson, "Stephen's Speech in Acts," 284.

focus not only on the *story* it tells (the "what") but also on the distinct *way* by which it is told (the "how").[8]

1. The Call and Promise of God (Acts 7:2-16)

The first portion of Stephen's speech focuses on Abraham and the patriarchs. God's call prompted Abraham to leave his family and travel to a different land (Acts 7:2-5). God promised Abraham that his descendants would be "enslaved and mistreated" in a "country not their own" (v. 6) but that they would return and worship God "in this place" that God promised to them (v. 7). Despite the patriarchs' jealousy of Joseph, "God was with him" (v. 9). As a result, God cared both for Joseph and for the patriarchs through him when famine ravaged the region (vv. 10-16). This attention on what God had done sets the stage for the unfolding story of Israel as God's people. Yet the wavering response of the patriarchs in their treatment of Joseph offers a clue to their lack of obedience to God's call and commandments, as seen throughout their history. This marks Stephen's contention as the speech unfolds.

> **In order to interpret Stephen's speech appropriately, a reader must focus not only on the *story* it tells (the "what") but also on the distinct *way* by which it is told (the "how").**

2. The Faithfulness of God (Acts 7:17-43)

The dominant role of Moses within this largest portion of Stephen's speech could easily lead one to conclude that Moses is the central character. To be sure, this portion of the speech has been expanded due to the inclusion of stories about Moses's birth and adulthood (see Acts 7:20-34). These accounts were probably included to reaffirm Moses as God's chosen representative for Israel.

But why would that reaffirmation be necessary? Note that the speech not

---

8. See this distinction between "story" and "discourse" within a narrative in chapter 2 of this book, pp. 33-34, which was first discussed by Chatman, *Story and Discourse*.

only offers a basic account of Israel's history but also assesses what happened within that history. The likely reason for reaffirming Moses as God's representative is that the rejection of God's representative is ultimately a rejection of God. Thus Stephen states that after Moses "received living words" for the people on Mount Sinai (v. 38), Israel's ancestors refused to obey Moses and rejected him. Stephen's speech reiterates that rejection in two ways. First, he describes the people as having "in their hearts turned back to Egypt" (v. 39; see Num. 14:3-4). Second, they requested Aaron to make them gods (Acts 7:40; Exod. 32:1-6). What was detestable in this idolatrous act was the demonstration of their belief that this golden calf could do for them what God had not done: lead them out of the wretched desert to salvation and safety.[9] In contrast to such rejection that celebrated "what their own hands had made" (Acts 7:41), Moses declared God to be faithful and that God would "raise up for you a prophet like me from your own people" (v. 37). Ultimately for the Lukan narrator, both the identity of this prophet and Israel's response (acceptance or rejection) are key aspects of the speech's message.

3. The Call to Worship God (Acts 7:44-50)

The mention of two tabernacles—of Molek (Acts 7:43) and of Israel (v. 44)—contrasts the differences in worship that confronted the ancestors of Israel and challenge the readers of Acts. Whereas the tabernacle of Molek was associated with the idolatrous worship of gods built with human hands (v. 43), the tabernacle of Israel that was built "according to the [divine] pattern" (v. 44) was associated with God's provision. Ironically, God provided this to Moses at the same time when the Israelites formed their idol, which underscores the futile and idolatrous nature of reliance on that which was "made by human hands" (v. 48). The speech offers a similar assessment of the temple for God that Solomon

---

9. See John J. Kilgallen, "The Speech of Stephen, Acts 7:2-53," *The Expository Times* 115, no. 9 (June 2004): 294.

erected. The adversative conjunction (*alla*) at the start of verse 48 makes it clear that God ("the Most High") will not "live in houses made by human hands" (v. 48). Such a renunciation, supported by the quotation of Isaiah 66:1-2, is not limited to the temple. This is a critique of any human or institutional attempt to place claims on God that ultimately limit God or diminish the greatness of God, since to worship God is to recognize God as the maker and source of "all these things" (Acts 7:50; Isa. 66:2).

4. Stephen's Charges against His Accusers (Acts 7:51-53)

The shift in tone at the end of the speech is noticeable in two distinct ways. First, most of Stephen's speech has offered only a general critique that could apply to the Jewish council. He invited his judges to join him (note the repeated "our ancestors"; see Acts 7:11-12, 15, 19, 38, 45) in considering their shared history as the chosen people of God. Second, the speech's tone changes from the first-person plural perspective (we) to an accusatory, second-person stance. That is, the accused (Stephen) now offered charges against his accusers, which essentially described *them* as guilty of idolatry and resistant to the Holy Spirit, thereby accusing them of associating with and continuing the sinful practices of their Jewish ancestors (v. 51). Such practices included the persecution and killing of God's prophets, which Stephen linked directly to the council's involvement in the death of Jesus (v. 52). So Stephen's point was simply this: those who gathered to judge whether he himself was speaking against the law had failed to keep it themselves, despite their affirmation of its divine authority (because it was "ordained by angels" [v. 53, NRSVue]).

> **Stephen's point was simply this: those who gathered to judge whether he himself was speaking against the law had failed to keep it themselves, despite their affirmation of its divine authority.**

The Confirmations of Stephen's Speech

The Lukan narrator indicates that both Stephen's murder and the subsequent persecution of the believers were direct responses to Stephen's speech. But since that narrator typically appropriates speeches for broader purposes within the Acts narrative, then one should also consider its function beyond the incident with Stephen.

In addition to there being parallels between the Stephen episode and two Lukan accounts of Jesus being rejected (Jesus at the synagogue in Nazareth [Luke 4:16-30] and Jesus's arrest and crucifixion [22:66–23:49]), a significant parallel episode occurs in Acts 21 (where Paul arrives in Jerusalem after the conclusion of his ministry). There are noteworthy similarities:

Acts 6–8	Acts 21
1. Stephen was wrongly accused (by false witnesses) about speaking against the law and temple (6:11, 13-14).	1. Paul was wrongly accused (by reports) about speaking against the law (v. 21) and also against the temple (v. 28).
2. Stephen appeared for a hearing before the Jewish council (6:15–7:1).	2. Paul appeared before the elders of the Jerusalem church (vv. 18-25).
3. Stephen offered his case in his speech (7:2-53).	3. Paul said nothing but submitted to the recommendation that he go through (and fund) a rite of purification at the temple (vv. 18-25).[10]
4. Stephen's accusers rejected his message, were enraged, and then murdered him (7:54–8:1).	4. Accusers of Paul captured him (before he completed the rite of purification at the temple) and tried to kill him (vv. 27-31). Later attempts to kill him ensued (see 23:12-22).

The similarities of these two episodes encourage readers to hold this portion of Acts together as a unit (regarding the expanding church beyond Jerusalem) and suggest that they read Stephen's speech as commentary on that material.

As commentary on the expanding ministry of the church, Stephen's speech includes several themes that help readers of Acts understand and interpret

---

10. This one difference among the similarities between these two passages may suggest (a) that the argument in Stephen's speech need not be repeated, (b) that Paul's actions "speak" for him in place of any direct speech, or (c) both of these options.

what God was doing through the mission of the church. First, God consistently called God's people to extend God's grace and saving purposes beyond "traditional" places, boundaries, and expectations. Such a call was at the heart of Israel's history. The call of Abraham drove him from his homeland with the seemingly impossible promise of God making a people from his descendants when Abraham and Sarah had no children. The call of the people of Israel out of Egyptian bondage stretched their imagination, which had become as rigid as the bricks they formed in the Egyptian desert, and sought to make them into a people known by God's name. What this speech reiterates is that God not only called and promised but also enabled God's people and their mission.

But second, what this speech also underscores from Israel's history is that the people repeatedly embraced idolatry, the worship of what their own hands made. The move from tabernacle to temple illustrates Israel's repeated attempts to domesticate God. They saw sacred sites and religious commandments as idols—as objects to maintain and manage rather than as means by which to love God and love neighbor. Their continued disobedience and lack of repentance were signs of their ongoing resistance to God's repeated calls to repentance, as God's prophets (such as Moses) had spoken to them as God led them.

Third, Stephen's speech offers an ongoing assessment (or perhaps a fresh story)[11] of the place of the Jewish temple and law. As the Christian movement continued to spread throughout the Mediterranean world as part of Judaism (and not separate from it), these questions would continue to rise to the surface. Stephen did not, as his accusers alleged, denounce the temple in Jerusalem or the Jewish law. But he was not silent about Israel's ongoing disobedience, which could be seen most readily throughout its history in its resistance and

---

11. See Michal Beth Dinkler, "The Politics of Stephen's Storytelling: Narrative Rhetoric and Reflexivity in Acts 7:2-53," *Zeitschrift für die neutestamentliche Wissenschaft und die Kunde der älteren Kirche* 111, no. 1 (2020): 33-64.

outright rejection of God's purposes. Stephen's speech reveals that the resistance and opposition the believers *also* faced from leaders in Jewish circles were a continuation of that dubious history. Such opposition was an indication that these religious leaders expected God to conform to the standards of their religious entities. Such attempts to domesticate God and to exercise authority over God and others contrasted with Luke's depiction of the believers in Acts, who worshiped God and embraced God's mission for the world.[12]

But this does not mean that Stephen's speech was meant merely as an indictment against those within Jewish circles who rejected the Christian gospel. When Acts was written, the religious and social dynamics that characterized the narrative within Acts had changed. It is likely that the Christian church had become increasingly separate from its original Jewish context and had become increasingly non-Jewish in its "membership." But the basic issues remained, just as they do today; Stephen's speech continues to speak to those who seek to read and interpret Acts to gain insight into how God continues to work and into the ongoing dangers to the church of domesticating God by our practices and our "correct" beliefs. Thus Stephen's speech keeps on speaking to those of the church who prayerfully read Acts as sacred Scripture.

Questions for Consideration

1. How do you explain the prominence (i.e., the length) of Stephen's speech within the broader Acts narrative?

2. What do you think might be the reasons for the focus of Stephen's speech, since it does not seem to address the accusations that led to his hearing?

3. How had the issue of idolatry been part of Israel's past? And in what ways was that message for the readers of Acts, not just for Stephen's audience?

---

12. See Thompson, *Keeping the Church*.

4. What do you understand as the connections between the themes and emphases of Stephen's speech and Acts?

5. What might be ways that contemporary persons and churches seek to domesticate God through their religious practices? Explain.

B. Summaries in Acts: Introduction

Along with speeches, perhaps the most distinctive aspect of the Acts narrative is the Lukan use of summary statements. In these statements, there is a distinctive shift from the description of specific scenes to statements or paragraphs that summarize activities or actions in general ways. These summary materials are rather distinctive in the Greek text, since the narration shifts from the aorist tense (which may, among other things, function as the historical tense) to the imperfect tense, which focuses on customary or repeated action. In the early chapters of Acts, the most notable examples of these summary sections are found in 2:42-47, 4:32-37, and 5:12-16.[1]

A question that has plagued scholars for the last century or so has to do with the reasons behind such a distinct shift in tone and style in these materials. There have been a couple of distinct ways that scholars have approached that question. One way has been to consider the sources that the Lukan author used to compose Acts. In many ways, the consideration of sources with regard to Acts is much more difficult than similar considerations with regard to, for instance, the Synoptic Gospels or even the books of the Pentateuch. In the case of the Synoptic Gospels, we have enough similar materials among the three

---

1. A cursory look at different English translations of the latter part of Acts 2 will reveal differences among them for the beginning of the summary section concluding the chapter. For instance, the NRSVue begins the final paragraph with verse 43, whereas the CEB and NIV include verse 42 in that final paragraph. The NRSVue seems to put more stock in the Greek verb beginning verse 43 (*ginomai*) that often begins a new section in narrative texts such as the Gospels and Acts. But the CEB and NIV recognize the shift in Greek verb tenses (from the aorist to the imperfect tense) in verses 42-47.

accounts that one can make some plausible conclusions about sources such as "Q" (although some persons are far more confident in things regarding "Q" than the evidence would suggest). In the case of the Pentateuch, numerous indications of differing perspectives exist within the narrative itself (e.g., two different creation accounts in Genesis) that point to the likelihood of multiple sources behind the composition of the final forms of these five books. However, in Acts, there is little tangible evidence to go on concerning sources, so source critics have tended to delineate the differences in the variety of materials.

Another approach that is more recent (from the mid-1900s) is really a methodological "cousin" to the source-critical method mentioned above. Redaction critics identified the distinctive stylistic shift in the summary materials as editorial work contributed by the Lukan author. In other words, the common general conclusion is that the materials describing specific scenes and situations in Acts came largely from a variety of sources available to the author, with the summary material exposing the editorial hand of that author in connecting those materials together. Thus, for example, the Pentecost materials preceding the last paragraph in Acts 2 and then those describing the healing of the lame man in Acts 3 came from multiple sources, with the Lukan author creating a summary paragraph as a transitional section connecting those scenes and materials together.

To be sure, both source critics and redaction critics have contributed significantly to the study of the biblical texts, including the Acts of the Apostles. Both approaches have helpfully analyzed the text of Acts and identified the different kinds of materials within that text. However, when the scholarly dust has settled, one must ask how such approaches have contributed to the interpretation of the summary materials in Acts. Generally speaking, there have been two conclusions about these materials. One conclusion, which is prevalent in scholarly circles and follows the work of source critics, is that the summary materials really contribute little to Acts, other than connecting the various materials and holding them together. Another conclusion, following the work of redaction critics, is that these materials reveal the theological tendencies of the author.

What more recent approaches such as narrative criticism have more helpfully noted is that both source criticism and redaction criticism inadequately account for these Lukan summary materials because both approaches only account for *portions* of the Acts narrative. That is, although both approaches contribute *in some ways* to the analysis and interpretation of Acts, the interpreter should not account for only a portion of a narrative, since, as narrative criticism contends, one must account for the features and details of a given narrative *holistically*. Thus the interpreter cannot simply ignore either the summary statements (as source critics generally do) or the Acts materials dependent on sources (as redaction critics generally do). Rather, one must account for *Acts*, and that means the entire Acts narrative.

When an interpreter examines the Lukan summary materials from a narrative-critical perspective (which takes into consideration the literary concerns and techniques of the Greco-Roman world), he or she finds that these materials offer a different approach to narration that correlates with the shift in Greek verb tenses. When the Lukan narrator describes scenes such as the Pentecost event and Peter's response to the crowd, that narrator offers an account that *shows* the reader what happened. Although there may be details that subtly or implicitly direct the reader's attention in certain kinds of ways, this kind of indirect description leaves it to the

> **When offering summary statements, the role of the narrator shifts from *showing* (or implicit, more subtle, description) to *telling* the reader explicitly about certain kinds of things.**

reader to fill in the gaps and to make appropriate conclusions. However, when offering summary statements, the role of the narrator shifts from *showing* (or implicit, more subtle, description) to *telling* the reader explicitly about certain kinds of things. That is, the narrator—who tends to hide behind the description of particular scenes and who leaves it to the reader to make the appropriate conclusion(s) about the described persons, scenes, and events—now steps out onto the narrative stage and tells the reader *directly* what is important to see. It is almost like the Lukan author comes out and says through these statements, "It is essential that you get this, so I am just going to tell you what is important here."

If this is how the Lukan summary statements might potentially function, then the interpreter of Acts needs to take seriously the specific place and role of these materials within the narrative. If the narrator includes these materials to give readers specific direction, then readers must give them adequate attention in the interpretive process. These are not merely the "narrative seam work" that holds Acts together. Rather, what we have here may be a type of material that should be understood as having a specific narrative function within the larger narrative structure of Acts.

5

Must I Tell You *Everything?* The Pentecost and Postarrest Summaries

(ACTS 2:42-47; 4:32-37)

Some persons cannot tell a good story. Yet others are *really good* storytellers! And the Lukan author was one of those persons who could tell an exceptionally good story. If one accepts the consensus about the author of the Third Gospel and Acts—that the same person wrote both books as a two-volume work—this author is responsible for some of the most memorable New Testament stories, including the birth of Jesus (Luke 2:1-20), the parables of the good Samaritan (10:27-39) and of the prodigal son (15:11-32), the encounter between Jesus and Zacchaeus the chief tax collector (19:1-10), the healing of the crippled man at the temple by Peter and John (Acts 3:1-26), and the Philippian jail incident with Paul and Silas (16:16-40). And these vivid episodes remain fixed in the minds of the readers of Acts, long after encountering them within the narrative.

But the author does not simply move from one story to the next. From time to time, especially in the first several chapters in Acts, Luke inserts summary statements or paragraphs into the narrative. Rather than offering readers episodic materials, his narrative style shifts to describe more general, conventional activity. And these materials point out to readers *specific* things that happened, unlike more episodic scenes that expect readers to connect the dots and figure out more of those conclusions for themselves. These summary materials seem to reflect a concern to *tell* readers what they need to see, unlike others scenes that merely *show* or offer them a different perspective. But together, scenes and summaries (and speeches) construct a narrative framework for readers that may give them a new and imaginative outlook about what God is doing, about who they are, and about what grace looks like.

The first two summary statements in Acts are very familiar to many readers of Acts because of the extraordinary images of the gathered believers. But a closer look at each of these statements within their contexts helps to uncover their narrative function. Rather than these statements offering some sort of blueprint for the ideal church or some basic ideas for the activities of a local church, these materials serve to guide readers' imaginations about the identity and nature of God's people.

The Pentecost Summary (Acts 2:42-47)

The first Lukan summary offers a generalized picture of the ongoing results of what God had done at Pentecost. Since the brief description of the outpouring of the Spirit and the subsequent speech from Peter both point to this event as the restoration of Israel as the people of God, from the first sentence (Acts 2:42) the narrator points out activities among the believers that are suggestive of the covenant between God and Israel. Three aspects of this summary stand out.

First, although translations typically depict or list four activities in verse 42 as parallel or "equal" items within the sentence, the Greek text structures them differently in two pairs. On the one hand, the first pair emphasizes that the believers were devoted to "the apostles' teaching" and to "the fellowship" (AT), which denotes both an aspect of worship and the community of believers. On the other hand, the second pair focuses on "the breaking of bread" and literally "the prayers" (AT), which reverses the order of the first pair to emphasize fellowship by eating together in the homes of other believers and worship practices pertaining to times of prayer.[1] Both pairs underscore the essential aspects of Israel's covenant with God: love to God and love to neighbor. Interestingly, the Lukan narrator *never* uses the word "love" here or anywhere else in Acts to describe such activities. Instead, the narrator offers basic descriptions of what this kind of love and covenantal practice looked like among the believers after God had fulfilled God's promises about the gift of the Spirit for God's people (perhaps because the image is more beneficial than merely saying that they now lived in covenantal ways).

> **Together, scenes and summaries (and speeches) construct a narrative framework for readers that may give them a new and imaginative outlook about what God is doing, about who they are, and about what grace looks like.**

Second, the believers cared for the needs of one another (vv. 44-45). The depiction of the believers sharing everything did not mean they pooled all their resources. Verse 45 clarifies that it was customary for them to sell property and possessions when necessary to care for "anyone who had need." These practices were consistent with Jesus's call to minister to the poor (see Luke 4:16-19; 6:20-36; 12:33-34; 18:18-30). But this also fulfilled what had been expected of the covenant people of God from the beginning: among them was to be no needy person (see Deut. 15:4, 11).

Third, the believers' practices extended beyond themselves. The Lukan narrator does not depict these Spirit-filled believers as an isolated group detached from others. Whereas Pentecost and its aftermath have often been described as the birthday of the Christian church, note that the believers continued to meet together in the temple in Jerusalem (Acts 2:46), just as they would have done prior to the extraordinary Pentecost event. That is, they continued their worship practices as faithful Jewish persons. And despite how most translations render verse 47, the believers both praised God and "demonstrated God's

---

1. See Thompson, *Acts*, 95.

goodness to everyone" (CEB).[2] Although this group of people had experienced the fulfillment of God's promises (through the gift of the Spirit), theirs was not an exclusive group. Their identity as the people of God extended beyond that experience and even their understanding of what God was doing. So they did not keep God's grace to themselves but shared it with others through how they lived.[3]

In many respects, this generalized picture after Pentecost provides a brief but powerful glimpse into the effects of God's work among the believers. Rather than understanding these images as guides or principles for imitation by all believers or churches, the summary offers a broader dynamic picture of the believers who, empowered by God's Spirit, embodied the original covenant with God as the people of God. Such a picture encourages readers of Acts to see and imagine themselves in fresh ways in light of the covenant with God, in contrast to the ideals and images of peoples and communities that surround them, past and present.

The Postarrest Summary (Acts 4:32-37)

The gathering of the believers immediately after the arrest (and release) of Peter and John reaffirms both their commitment to the faith and the significance of that faith community. That the narrator describes the group as literally "their own" (Acts 4:23) contrasts them with the intimidating, powerful group of the Jewish council that threatened them not long before (vv. 5-22). It is no wonder their prayers for boldness resulted in answered prayers (see v. 31)!

The second Acts summary, which follows that scene, is often associated with the Pentecost summary because of their similarity in content. However, there

---

2. Most translations follow the "direction" of the KJV, which renders this portion of the verse as the believers "having favour with all the people" (e.g., see the NIV: "enjoying the favor of all the people"). However, both the Greek text and the context suggest the CEB translation to be a stronger one. See T. David Andersen, "The Meaning of *Echontes Charin Pros* in Acts 2.47," *New Testament Studies* 34 (1988): 604-10.

3. The Greek word translated "favor" (KJV, NASB, NIV) or "goodness" (CEB) in Acts 2:47 is *charis*, which is also translated "grace."

are also differences here due to its unique literary context. What is different about this particular summary is its emphasis on the ongoing witness of the apostles (v. 33), which corresponds with the context and the believers' prayer, so that God enabled the entire group to speak with boldness (see vv. 29, 31). The Lukan narrator points out that the apostles' testimony was about "the resurrection of the Lord Jesus" (v. 33). That is, they did *exactly* what the Jewish council warned them *not* to do!

But the narrator connects the apostles' acts of witnessing with descriptions about the believers' care for one another. These descriptions are reminiscent of the images of believers after Pentecost. The depiction of the believers as being of "one heart and soul" (NRSVue) highlights the common bond among them that enabled them to share possessions with one another (v. 32). The reiteration that there was "not a needy person among them" (v. 34, NRSVue) celebrates the elimination of need among God's people because of God's blessing (see Deut. 15:4), which was made possible by those who, from time to time, liquidated assets and brought the proceeds to the apostles for use within the community of believers (Acts 4:34-35). Such connections between the communal care for others and the proclamation of the gospel once again remind readers of the covenantal aspects of the people of God.

The narrator's mention of believers who sold property to care for the needs of others (and the identification of Barnabas as an example of such benefaction) encourages the readers of Acts to envisage how such actions would have been startling and countercultural in that day (vv. 34*b*-37). Although those believers with property would have been wealthy and in the minority, the Lukan description of their donation is a radical departure from customary social practices. The picture of wealthy believers placing the proceeds of the sale of property at the apostles' feet would have them kneeling before those with lower social status. Here was a wealthy, powerful landowner bowing before lowly Galilean fishermen (and others)!

Conventional practice would have required that the wealthy *receive* honor from the apostles, and yet these believers took the contrary position of humility before those who assumed the role of leaders among them because these leaders were Jesus's witnesses. By giving the funds to the apostles for distribution rather than distributing the funds themselves, the wealthy also relinquished all social expectations of receiving something in return from those they assisted.[4] Such descriptions seek to help readers of Acts imagine fresh and creative ways to care for one another as the people of God that are not constrained by society's expectations and limitations.

The summary's insertion prior to the episode involving Ananias and Sapphira suggests that the summary functions within the narrative as a way to interpret the couple's actions. By all outward appearances, their actions seem identical to those of Barnabas: They, like Barnabas, owned property and sold it. And they, like Barnabas, brought proceeds from the sale and placed them at the apostles' feet (5:1-2; see 4:37). However, the narrator offers two additional details that change the perspective on that scene: Ananias withheld part of the proceeds from the sale of the property (with Sapphira's knowledge), and then he brought the remainder of the funds to the apostles (5:2).

By not providing clarification behind Peter's charge that Ananias was guilty of lying to the Holy Spirit (v. 3) and to God (v. 4), the Lukan narrator leaves the reader to determine what may have caused the untimely death of Ananias (v. 5) and later his wife (v. 10). Because the contrast between Barnabas and the couple focuses only on what persons could witness through actions, the narrator offers no *direct* attention on matters of intention and motivation behind those actions (which is consistent with ancient narratives), except for Peter's charge. And even the charge itself suggests that first the property and later the funds from its sale belonged to Ananias (and perhaps to Sapphira) to manage as they wished (see v. 4).

---

4. See Bruce J. Malina and John J. Pilch, *Social-Science Commentary on the Book of Acts* (Minneapolis: Fortress, 2008), 46-47.

So where is the problem? Interpreters have often suggested that Ananias and Sapphira were guilty of deception. That is, they pretended to do what Barnabas and others had done because they wanted the notability that came with being like them. The problem with such an interpretation is that persons would *never* have had such aspirations, since those actions essentially flipped the prevailing social script for the sake of others. Such actions were so radical and countercultural that persons would never *aspire* to renounce their social status before those whose status was beneath their own, and they certainly would not pretend to do such things that flew in the face of everything that culture valued. Thus it is possible that the couple simply went along with what others had done, not for notability or pretense, but because they thought it was "the thing to do."

But their hearts were not in it. One can make the argument that their contribution would help others who were in need. And one can also contend that they assisted and "loved others" in that manner. But by withholding part of the proceeds, they also withheld themselves from the rest of the believers. Although they had extended assistance (and love) toward others, such benevolence and loving action were only one directional. By holding on to those resources for themselves, the couple not only sought their own security apart from the community but also withheld opportunity for others to love and care *for them*. As a result, their actions would never strengthen or enhance their own relationships within the community of believers. Perhaps this is what was behind Peter's charge: their actions suggested or hinted at covenant (with God and others), but it was based on a hoax. This might also explain Sapphira's surprise upon hearing about her husband's death, since no one present was even mourning his loss (see v. 7).

Perhaps this explains why the Lukan narrator describes the death of both Ananias and Sapphira as he does. Often, interpreters focus on who was responsible for their demise and whether this was a story of divine judgment.[5] But the verb used to depict their deaths (*ekpsychō*) suggests that these two—whose actions appeared like those of this community, which the Lukan narrator described as being of "one heart and soul" (4:32, NRSVue)—had actually become *soulless* by making themselves outsiders of that same community.[6] Yet even with this episode, readers of Acts encounter a fresh perspective that encourages them to consider what a dynamic community of believers looks like with God as their creative source. Such a perspective challenges us to see how often our so-called love of neighbor has been similar to that of Ananias and Sapphira. We are willing to give from what is essentially our surplus to help another, and yet we never allow ourselves to get into a position where we can accept such love in return, because we avoid such lateral, mutual relationships. What the Lukan narrator offers is an alternative picture of a faithful community of God's people that is open to whatever opportunities and relationships that love makes available to them.

Summaries and the Narrative of Acts

Although the summaries in Acts have often been interpreted as guides for imitation, readers of Acts should see how these materials function within the narrative itself. As speeches function as implicit commentary to guide readers in their interpretation of what has happened and will be encountered in the narrative, summaries function similarly but in more direct ways to guide the reader. Unlike the general tendency for the narrative to show readers what happened (which requires them to connect the dots and make more conclusions themselves), summaries allow the narrator to tell readers more directly about what happened and to emphasize specific themes and issues as they relate to

---

5. See J. Albert Harrill, "Divine Judgment against Ananias and Sapphira (Acts 5:1-11): A Stock Scene of Perjury and Death," *Journal of Biblical Literature* 130, no. 2 (2011): 351-69.

6. Given this interpretation of the Ananias and Sapphira episode, the context suggests that the response of the believers to what happened (*phobos megas*) should be translated "great awe" (AT) rather than "great fear" (Acts 5:5), because of God's presence among them. See Thompson, *Acts*, 133.

the narrative. But this requires both careful attention to the literary context and openness to the imaginative directions of the guidance provided by these summaries.

Questions for Consideration

1. How would you describe narrative summaries as found in Acts? And how are they different from typical episodes within the narrative?

2. What do you identify as key aspects of the Pentecost summary at the end of Acts 2? How do these relate to the materials in chapter 2? In the chapters that follow?

3. What do you identify as key aspects of the postarrest summary at the end of Acts 4? How do these relate to the materials in chapter 4? In chapter 5?

4. Read another Lukan summary, Acts 5:12-16. After reading it, what do you identify as key aspects of that summary? How does this summary relate to the Ananias and Sapphira episode? To the rest of chapter 5?

C. Characterization in Acts: Introduction[1]

Perhaps the two most important features of an ancient story are its plot and characters. On the one hand, the plot[2] is simply the arrangement and unfolding of the story's action. Aristotle emphasized the importance of the connection of the story's action from beginning to end and compared the importance of each part of a work to that of a living organism.[3] Such action is the most important part of any narrative. On the other hand, the narrative's characters carry out or embody that action. And readers are often drawn into a story, sometimes because they relate to a particular character and sometimes because they disapprove of some qualities of a character.[4]

Readers can quickly see the two distinct aspects or levels of a narrative when encountering characters in the narrative itself. On the story level (the "what" of the narrative), readers will immediately see what persons are involved in the action and what they are doing. But when readers step back to consider what the narrator has done with those characters by describing them in particular ways (not to mention what has not been included in those descriptions), they

---

1. For a more detailed treatment of this topic, see Thompson, *Keeping the Church*, 17-28. For a collection of essays that explore characterization in Luke-Acts, see Frank E. Dicken and Julia A. Snyder, eds., *Characters and Characterization in Luke-Acts*, Library of New Testament Studies 548 (New York: T. and T. Clark, 2016).

2. The Greek word translated "plot" is *mythos*, from which is derived the English term "myth."

3. See Aristotle, *Poetics* 7.1-10; 8.1-4.

4. See Brown, *Gospels as Stories*, 65, who notes that the character Ebenezer Scrooge in Charles Dickens's novel *A Christmas Carol* functions through most of the book as a foil, since his extreme callous and selfish behavior is the opposite of how readers would expect him to behave. However, the transformation at the end, which results in a generous and caring spirit, also draws readers to this character.

have now entered into the realm of characterization, which is part of the discourse level (the "how" of the narrative). Thus characterization may be defined as the art of bringing characters in a story to life in a unique way *(a)* through what they do and say and *(b)* in relation to one another.[5]

What this simply means is that the various characters who populate the Acts narrative come to life largely through the actions, speeches, conversations, and interactions with other characters that the Lukan narrator has included as part of the broader story. Along the way, some qualities have been underscored, while others have been minimized. Some actions have been placed before readers for their attention, and other events and activities receive only a glance. Yet all of these are part of the Lukan author's hand in shaping the work, based on his theological perspective and purpose. So considering how characters are depicted—not in isolation but in relation to one another and as part of the broader plot—is essential to reading Acts as narrative. Given this, interpreters of Acts should remember several aspects of ancient characterization as they read, interpret, and engage this narrative.

> **The various characters who populate the Acts narrative come to life largely through the actions, speeches, conversations, and interactions with other characters that the Lukan narrator has included as part of the broader story.**

First, recognize the variety of characters that appear in the narrative. Some characters appear with little or no development and seem relegated to a function within the plot (e.g., those who accused the believers at Pentecost of being intoxicated [Acts 2:13]). These "simple" characters highlight a basic quality and seem to disappear as the narrative moves on. But other more developed characters remain longer within the narrative, are observed more fully both in action and speech, and end up interacting with other characters and narrative emphases, so their place and significance are more nuanced. Thus readers should not conflate

---

5. Cf. ibid., 65-66.

flat characters with these other "rounder" characters who have a larger narrative role and perhaps receive more narrative description and attention.

Second, assess the actions and speech of characters in relation to characterization. The indirect description of a character through action is the primary means by which ancient authors presented characters. This means of characterization relies mostly on what characters say and do within the narrative to "develop" those characters, both positively and negatively, not on other matters found in more contemporary literature (such as the appearance or age of the characters). These actions tend to reflect matters of significance, including a person's choice, intention, and "character."[6] Narratives like Acts and the Gospels tend to rely on indirect descriptions to depict most characters.

Third, consider the role of explicit or direct means of describing characters. There are instances when the narrator provides additional information about a character that readers may need in order to evaluate specific actions or a specific scene. Such information may come in the form of a summary statement or paragraph that does not *show* readers about a scene or event but *tells* them specific things that happened over a period of time. These explicit statements may also offer insights and some basic conclusions *from the Lukan narrator himself* about motives, emotions, or thoughts (that is, information about characters not readily accessible to someone observing them) that directly inform readers about specific actions or events in the narrative. The narrator may even describe something about the character's social status, gender, vocation, or appearance.[7] Since such insights are relatively rare in ancient literature, such direct means of communication suggest their importance from the author's perspective.

Fourth, note how different characters interact with one another in various scenes and episodes throughout Acts. No character stands alone within a scene

---

6. The word "character" is placed within quotation marks to distinguish it from the character of a narrative. In ancient discussions, the Greek term *ethos* was the term that would be used here for "character." See, e.g., Aristotle, *Poetics* 6.7-8.

7. See Brown, *Gospels as Stories*, 72.

or the broader story. In many ways, narrative characters often reveal *other* characters in the story as their interactions result in new actions as well as both comparisons and contrasts between them. Such interactions contribute to the ways that readers may see and assess these characters. As a result, the various ways that characters interact also provide imaginative space for the readers of Acts in their quest to interpret the narrative.

6

Philip and the Ethiopian Eunuch: Perspectives about Believers and the Church

(ACTS 8:26-40)

The Lukan narrator introduces his readers to a broad range of characters throughout the Acts narrative. There are Jewish religious leaders in Jerusalem who distanced themselves from the fledgling Jesus movement (as mentioned in the previous chapter). There are rogue Jewish exorcists in Ephesus who claimed authority over evil spirits in Jesus's name, only to have their duplicity exposed for all to see (Acts 19:13-17). Luke depicts persons who were enthralled by Paul and Barnabas and who sought to honor them as the Greek gods Hermes and Zeus by offering sacrifices to them (see 14:11-13). Luke also describes others who thought (correctly) that believers like Paul were disruptors of their way of life and sought to stop them with legal charges and incarceration (see, e.g., 16:16-40; 17:16-34; 19:23-40). At other times, readers find the accused Paul before Roman officials, whom the narrator depicts as unreliable, incompetent in dealing with Paul's case, or more interested in favors and bribes than in serving as the legal "overseer" for that case (see 24:1-27; 25:1-12; 25:13–26:32).

The story of Philip and the Ethiopian eunuch is noteworthy for several reasons. First, it pairs two very distinct characters, whom the Lukan narrator characterizes very differently. Second, the story relies on limited action (and thus largely on interaction) between the two characters. But its placement within the narrative (where the gospel and church were beginning to extend beyond Jerusalem and traditional Jewish settings to people whom the Jewish religious establishment considered to be outsiders) suggests that readers should watch for a backstory or another message in addition to the more obvious action between them. Third, the episode itself tends to be an ignored episode within the reading and interpretation of Acts. Perhaps this is because the lack of action would force persons into public conversations about the characters themselves and most persons—both ancient and contemporary—would rather not talk about a eunuch![1]

However, the inclusion of this episode with these unique characters invites readers to examine it more closely. And the assessment of the depiction of these two characters can help readers discern the function and potential message of this episode within the broader Acts narrative.

The Characterization of Philip

The Lukan depiction of Philip in this episode is dependent on what the narrator has already offered his readers. Luke first introduced Philip in Acts 6. After a problem arose within the growing community of believers in Jerusalem over the care for widows, Philip was one of seven persons selected to assist the apostles by taking on the responsibility of that ministry. This was done so that the apostles could give their attention "to prayer and the service of proclaiming the word" (v. 4, CEB). According to Luke, the believers based the selection of these "deacons" (from the Greek word *diakonia*, meaning "ministry") on three stated criteria: (1) the seven were to be men (*andras* [males]) from the larger

---

1. See Bruce J. Malina, *The New Testament World: Insights from Cultural Anthropology* (Atlanta: John Knox, 1981), 2: "Eunuchs are hardly the topic of our dinner-time conversations, much less the object of prolonged sermonizing in our churches."

group of believers, (2) each of them should have a good reputation, and (3) each of them must be "full of the Spirit and wisdom" (v. 3). Of the seven who were selected, Luke adds additional material about only Stephen (the first mentioned) and Nicolas (the last mentioned). That Philip's name appears second (after Stephen's) is likely due to his appearance within the Acts narrative after the hearing and stoning of Stephen (at the end of Acts 7).

The appearance of Philip in Samaria serves as the first narrative example of what happened to the scattered believers in Acts. The Lukan narrator mentions nothing about the motive behind Philip's preaching. That is, nothing explicit suggests that Philip followed divine guidance. Rather, Philip (and many others) went where the persecution after Stephen's death scattered them, and they proclaimed the gospel message "wherever they went" (8:4; see vv. 1-4). Although Philip landed among Samaritans (a group neither Jewish nor Gentile but in between), who were notorious for their centuries-long hostile "relationship" with the Jewish people,[2] the extraordinary supernatural signs and the positive responses from the people depict both him and his ministry favorably (vv. 6-8, 12).

Although the Lukan narrator mysteriously mentions nothing more about Philip in Samaria (vv. 14-25), the narrator reintroduces him briefly at the beginning of the new episode (v. 26). What the narrator clearly describes is the divine guidance behind Philip's actions in two distinct ways. First, Philip received specific instructions from "an angel of the Lord" (v. 26), not only conveying when and where to go[3] but also nudging him to relocate from a place of successful ministry to a remote location that may seem to have little potential. The simple assertion that "he got up and went" (v. 27, NRSVue), with no mention of any objections, offers the reader a picture of someone obedient to God's direction.

---

2. See Thompson, *Acts*, 174-75.

3. The Greek expression translated "go south" (NIV) or "at noon" (CEB) may actually connote both ideas, despite the limitations of English translations that focus on only one aspect. See Thompson, *Acts*, 181.

Second, Philip received additional guidance upon encountering the Ethiopian eunuch, who was seated in his chariot or carriage (v. 28). Luke states that the Spirit told Philip to approach the man's chariot and "stay near it" (v. 29). Luke could have merely stated that Philip approached the chariot as instructed; his description of a running Philip is reminiscent of the prophet Elijah (1 Kings 18:46). Thus the Lukan narrator has characterized Philip positively as God's servant who has faithfully proclaimed the gospel of Jesus Christ wherever he went and to whomever he met. This characterization is consistent with Peter's reiteration of Joel 2:32, that "*everyone* who calls on the name of the Lord will be saved" (Acts 2:21; emphasis added). Thus the divine guidance that has led Philip to this new location should encourage readers to anticipate what God might do next in this scene.

The Characterization of the Ethiopian Eunuch

Although Luke's depiction of Philip helps readers see Philip as a *specific* person or individual, the characterization of the Ethiopian eunuch is much more dependent on *general* character traits and assumptions that readers would associate with persons like him. Since the narrator directly mentions several things about this person, readers must consider how these contribute to the overall portrayal of the Ethiopian eunuch.

First, the Lukan narrator mentions that he was "a man of Ethiopia" (Acts 8:27, AT). For ancient readers, two perceptions were associated with the nation of Ethiopia.[4] One perception was that this nation was a far-off land on the fringe of the empire. Persons commonly saw Ethiopia as part of "the ends of the earth" (cf. 1:8).[5] Because Ethiopia exported treasured commodities to the empire—spices and incense, ivory, ebony, and gold—people viewed the land as

---

4. It should be noted that this reference to Ethiopia is believed to include most of modern Ethiopia and Sudan.
5. See Homer, *Iliad* 23.205-97; Herodotus, *Histories* 3.114-15; Strabo, *Geography* 1.2.24-28.

an exotic location beyond their own inhabited world. A second perception was of the Ethiopian people themselves. Because of their origin from an unknown, distant land as well as their differences in appearance (e.g., in skin color), it was common for persons of the empire to see Ethiopians with suspicion, even considering them as morally deficient.[6] For instance, the first-century Greek geographer Strabo characterized Ethiopians with other "barbarians" as those who were "defective and inferior . . . due to their geographical location on the 'extremities of the inhabited world.'"[7] Because of such prevalent perceptions associated with Ethiopians among those of the Mediterranean world, it is doubtful that readers' initial impressions were favorable toward this ultimate "outsider." Rather, they would have seen him much as the Jewish people would have viewed the Samaritans with whom Philip found himself (8:5-25).

Second, the Lukan narrator identifies the man as a "eunuch" (v. 27). Of all descriptions, Luke uses this word repeatedly when referring to the man (also vv. 34, 36, 38-39). Interestingly, Luke never provides the man's name (unlike Philip or many other characters in Acts) but uses the designation "eunuch" as the primary means to identify him.[8] Some contend that this term was merely a reference to an "important official"[9] and not a "physical eunuch."[10] But this is unlikely for several reasons. One reason is that, since the next word (after the term "eunuch") explains the man's "official" role, an understanding of the

---

6. See Mikeal C. Parsons, *Body and Character in Luke and Acts: The Subversion of Physiognomy in Early Christianity* (Grand Rapids: Baker Academic, 2006), 132; Marianne B. Kartzow and Halvor Moxnes, "Complex Identities: Ethnicity, Gender and Religion in the Story of the Ethiopian Eunuch (Acts 8:26-40)," *Religion and Theology* 17 (2010): 191-93; Brittany E. Wilson, "'Neither Male nor Female': The Ethiopian Eunuch in Acts 8.26-40," *New Testament Studies* 60, no. 3 (2014): 411-17; and Gay L. Byron, *Symbolic Blackness and Ethnic Difference in Early Christian Literature* (New York: Routledge, 2002), 29-51.

7. Strabo, *Geography* 17.2.1. See also Diodorus Siculus 3.8.1-3; Pliny, *Natural History* 2.80.189-90.

8. Cf. Wilson, "Neither Male nor Female," 405: "Luke's repeated designation of the character as 'the eunuch' suggests that this designation is central and should thus be the guiding principle in our interpretation."

9. Some draw this conclusion because the Septuagint describes the married official Potiphar as a eunuch (Gen. 39:1). However, the Septuagint also depicts Potiphar as a *spadōn* (official) in Genesis 37:36. However, note that first-century Jewish writers like Philo understood Potiphar to be a physical eunuch (see, e.g., Philo, *Joseph* 37, 58-60; *Allegorical Interpretation* 3.236).

10. I use "physical eunuch" because there are two types of eunuchs: "intentionally" castrated males (not necessarily voluntary, as this was often done without consent) and "naturally" castrated males (at birth or caused by accident).

term "eunuch" merely as an "official" would seem redundant. Another reason is that the eunuch served the Ethiopian queen, and those who served queens in the ancient world were typically selected for that service *because* they were physical eunuchs. One additional reason is that Jewish scriptural texts refer to the inclusion of physical eunuchs in the last days (see Isa. 56:3-5).

However, despite the prominent role of some eunuchs in royal circles, eunuchs in the ancient world belonged to one of the most despised groups of people within society. Some were slaves whose condition was the result of punishment or oppression. But even those who were fortunate enough to attain powerful or influential positions (as in the case of Candace's treasurer) in that era could not escape the stigma that came with their unique condition. One may find the evidence of the condemnation of eunuchs in multiple ancient contexts: in the broader general context of antiquity,[11] but also more specifically in Jewish contexts.[12] In most cases, the basis for such criticism was the eunuch's uncertain (or ambiguous) gender status. Because others perceived eunuchs as "un-manned" men, one could argue that these persons had one foot in the realm of "women" and one foot in the realm of "men," which upset ancient cultural norms and raised suspicions among the populace.[13]

Luke, thus, on the one hand, depicts the eunuch before Philip and the readers of Acts as someone who had been "utterly stripped of honor, a monstrous incarnation of shame."[14] On the other hand, Luke also describes the

---

11. See, e.g., Herodotus, *Histories* 8.104-6; Lucian, *Eunuch* 6-11.

12. The exclusion of eunuchs is mandated in Deuteronomy 23:1: "No one whose testicles are crushed or whose penis is cut off shall come into the assembly of the Lord" (NRSVue). Additional legislation describes eunuchs among the blemished and ritually impure, as well as unfit for priestly service (Lev. 21:20; cf. 22:24). Two first-century Jewish authors, Josephus and Philo, reinforced the biblical stances toward eunuchs. Josephus described eunuchs as those "who have deprived themselves of their manhood" and their ability to procreate (*Jewish Antiquities* 4.290-91). He did not consider that many eunuchs were made eunuchs against their will. Similarly, Philo wrote about those banished from the sacred assembly, including those "who have suffered any injury or mutilation in their most important members" (*On the Special Laws* 1.324-25).

13. See Wilson, "Neither Male nor Female," 406-7.

14. F. Scott Spencer, "The Ethiopian Eunuch and His Bible: A Social-Science Analysis," *Biblical Theology Bulletin* 22, no. 4 (Winter 1992): 158.

eunuch as lacking a sense of place in God's created order, because his ambiguous gender identity ("neither male nor female"; see Philo, *Dreams* 2.184) and his "defective" anatomy embodied an impurity that was, from an ancient Jewish perspective, understood as contrary to God's wholeness and holiness.[15] So the repeated word "eunuch" in this passage in Acts 8 reinforces what readers of Acts would already assume: this eunuch was the ultimate outsider. And questions about whether he was a Jew or Gentile mattered little, perhaps because he was no better off than the Samaritans in the previous section (which also gives hope).[16]

Third, the remaining descriptions of the eunuch highlight various aspects of this person's status and affluence, and they contribute further to the ambiguous nature of his characterization in Acts. The mention of his "official" role as responsible for the entire treasury of "the Candace, the queen of the Ethiopians" (v. 27, NRSVue) indicates both his status and prominence within the Ethiopian palace. Because of past conflicts between Ethiopia and Rome in Egypt, one should not be surprised that both Ethiopia and its queen were regarded as dangers to Rome.[17] But two matters accentuate his wealth and status: his lounging in a "chariot" (NIV, NRSVue) or "carriage" (CEB), presumably accompanied by attendants, and his reading of the prophet Isaiah (Acts 8:28). Only a small percentage of persons were literate, and even fewer had the financial means to possess a personal copy of the scroll of Isaiah's work. The eunuch's pilgrimage to Jerusalem may have sparked his interest in Isaiah, especially since, as a eunuch, he was probably denied access to parts of the temple. Despite the cumulative effect of the various negative aspects of the Lukan depiction of the eunuch, which are based on general assumptions that readers of Acts would bring to the

---

15. See Parsons, *Body and Character*, 135-36, and Spencer, "Ethiopian Eunuch," 158-59.

16. See Scott Shauf, "Locating the Eunuch: Characterization and Narrative Context in Acts 8:26-40," *Catholic Biblical Quarterly* 71, no. 4 (October 2009): 762-75.

17. See Kartzow and Moxnes, "Complex Identities," 195-96.

table, these last images offer a glimpse into the eunuch as a religious person, which gives readers reason for hope as Philip approaches him.

The Interaction between Philip and the Ethiopian Eunuch

Because the Spirit's guidance orchestrated the meeting between Philip and the eunuch, readers should anticipate the topic of the ensuing conversation. After all, the narrator had already depicted Philip proclaiming the gospel of Jesus Christ (see Acts 8:5, 12). So it is no surprise that he began with the passage that was before the eunuch and "proclaimed the good news about Jesus" (v. 35, CEB).

But why was this man reading Isaiah? That is, why would this man turn to the prophet Isaiah when there were other scriptural texts (e.g., Torah and Psalms) that he could read and to which he could listen for God's Spirit to speak? Perhaps the answer is found in the specific passage that Luke quotes in this account. Perhaps the eunuch, whom society and even readers of Acts perceived as worthless and treated with contempt, gravitated to *this* portion of prophetic Scripture because it describes a figure to which he could relate: pitiful, slaughtered and left for dead, voiceless, completely humiliated, ostracized (see Acts 8:32; Isa. 53:7-8). To be sure, the eunuch could relate to this picture, since what this passage described paralleled his own life story. But as much as this text attracted the eunuch's attention, it also confused him.

This is where Philip's role as interpreter and proclaimer of the good news about Jesus came in (Acts 8:34-35). Luke does not repeat here what readers of Acts have already encountered earlier in the narrative: that Jesus of Nazareth, like the figure in Isaiah, was humiliated by death on a Roman cross. But that was not the end of the matter. Death did not get the final word, since this disgraced and humiliated one was taken or lifted up in exaltation and honor (see

1:2, 9-11; 2:24-36; 3:13-16, 22-26; 13:28-37; 26:22-23). What is such good news is not only that life redeems death but also that exaltation transforms humiliation and that honor replaces shame. And this is what the prophet Isaiah promised that God would someday accomplish among God's people, even for outsiders like eunuchs:

> Don't let the immigrant who has joined with the LORD say,
>
> > "The LORD will exclude me from the people."
>
> And don't let the eunuch say,
>
> > "I'm just a dry tree."
>
> The LORD says:
>
> > To the eunuchs who keep my sabbaths,
> >
> > choose what I desire,
> >
> > and remain loyal to my covenant.
> >
> > In my temple and courts, I will give them
> >
> > a monument and a name better than sons and daughters.
> >
> > I will give to them an enduring name
> >
> > that won't be removed. (Isa. 56:3-5, CEB)

The Lukan description of the baptism of the Ethiopian eunuch in the concluding paragraph focuses on the ironic aspects of this event. On the one hand, the narrator reiterates that the person seeking baptism (and therefore inclusion within the church as the people of God) really is a eunuch (Acts 8:36, 38-39).[18] Such references reinforce that others have perceived and treated the man as an outsider. Thus, like the Samaritans who appeared before this episode (vv. 5-25), the Jewish people would have regarded him as unworthy of inclusion among their ranks. On the other hand, by asking the question, "What is to prevent me from being baptized?" (v. 36, NRSVue), the eunuch pressed the issue that he

---

18. Note that the Lukan narrator uses the term "eunuch" only two other times in the rest of the broader passage (Acts 8:27, 34).

consistently faced from others. And at the heart of that issue was his exclusion from a people, from worship, from salvation, and from grace. Perhaps others had cited the passages from the Torah (e.g., Lev. 21:20; 22:24; Deut. 23:1) as justification for such exclusion and treatment.[19] Yet even with this background, the eunuch's question also indirectly expressed his understanding of the gospel about Jesus Christ: that Jesus's death and resurrection made it possible for the ultimate outsider to be incorporated into the people of God (see Acts 2:42-47; 8:5-8, 12-13).

Interestingly, Luke mentions nothing about the specifics of Philip's comments to the eunuch or even what the eunuch confessed.[20] Rather, the emphasis is on the eunuch's "trust embodied in seeking baptism in the middle of the wilderness."[21] Although his condition as a eunuch remained and would have caused others to continue to see him with suspicion (note that the narrator also describes him as a eunuch *after* his baptism; see 8:39), his baptism signified the common Lukan theme of inclusion into the church as part of the faithful people of God. And two simple expressions depicting his departure (v. 39) mirror other believers in Acts: he went "on his way" (as believers are described as people "on the Way"), suggesting he would return home to testify about his new Christian faith, and he was rejoicing, a common response in the Third Gospel and Acts to the new things that God was doing (see, e.g., Luke 1:14; 2:10; 15:5; 19:6; Acts 3:8; 5:41; 8:8; 13:48; 15:31). Thus the man left as still a eunuch—*and* yet now was also part of the church.

---

19. Although the Lukan narrator mentions nothing about this, readers may suspect from the eunuch's question (about who might prevent him from baptism [Acts 8:36]) that the eunuch heard from people, perhaps during his latest trip to Jerusalem, about the biblical passages that kept or prevented him from worship at the temple.

20. Textual variants include such possibilities that the KJV included (see Acts 8:37: "And Philip said, 'If you believe with all your heart, you may.' And he replied, 'I believe that Jesus Christ is the Son of God'" [AT]). But the best manuscripts omit this. See Bruce M. Metzger, *A Textual Commentary on the Greek New Testament*, 2nd ed. (New York: United Bible Societies, 1994), 315.

21. Barreto, "Gospel on the Move," 184.

Readers Interacting Imaginatively with Scripture

Both this episode and its context engage readers—past and present—to interact and reflect imaginatively on what they see and hear in this passage. This is because the Lukan author was not interested merely in reporting what happened between Philip and this high-ranking governmental official from a distant country. And it is doubtful that the author would be satisfied with contemporary readers concluding that this was just a divinely orchestrated encounter between two persons in the early decades of the fledgling Christian movement. Rather, the context of this episode (among other scenes that describe how the good news about Jesus Christ includes so many who had been excluded or marginalized by the prevailing Jewish traditions and institutions of that era) suggests something about how Luke may have wanted us as readers to interact with these stories.

But if we read these stories and the broader Acts narrative in the ways they were crafted, then the purpose behind an episode, like Philip's encounter with the Ethiopian eunuch, is not merely about how ancient Jewish traditions and institutions worked as exclusive entities. Rather, these narratives invite us into the story so that we may begin to imagine the ways that our *own* religious (Christian) institutions and practices—our churches, our favorite activities, our conversations, and so on—often function in

> These narratives invite us into the story so that we may begin to imagine the ways that our *own* religious (Christian) institutions and practices—our churches, our favorite activities, our conversations, and so on—often function in ways that treat individuals and groups as outsiders.

ways that treat individuals and groups as outsiders. What this episode encourages us to see is that persons and groups may be sitting or standing before us—persons whom we have already characterized in our minds (as readers of Acts had probably done with the Ethiopian eunuch) because of preconceptions that we place on them—who need a Philip to run or walk or sit with them as they are. It may mean coming to grips with the realization that, like the eunuch, their baptism may not change some things we thought it might, and yet it may mean embracing what God is doing in their lives—and ours (note that God guided Philip in this passage).

Stories and narratives like Acts do not seek to provide us with all the answers to our questions, but they do encourage faithful readers of Scripture to imagine what God might do when they not only trust God but also have eyes that watch for evidence of God at work, even in those they least expected. Our fears (that often dictate our characterization of others) do not have the final word, but God and God's grace do.

Questions for Consideration

1. When thinking about Philip in this episode, what characteristics stand out as most significant for you? Why?

2. What positive and/or negative aspects about the Ethiopian eunuch stand out for you as most influential when reading this episode? Why?

3. Identify the parts of the passage from Isaiah with which you think the Ethiopian eunuch most identified. What passages in some of the speeches (or preaching) in Acts may provide clues to Philip's own proclamation of the gospel about Jesus?

4. What do you think is behind the Ethiopian eunuch's question about baptism? What was/is the significance of baptism? How might he have experienced hindrances or persons preventing such inclusion?

5. What is the significance of the eunuch still being identified as a eunuch after baptism? What might that have said in its original context? What might this suggest in our own day?

6. How does this passage help the church think and imagine differently about how to respond to persons and groups who are often treated and viewed as outsiders?

7

"Who's That Knocking at the Door?": Peter, Rhoda, and the Jerusalem Prayer Meeting

(ACTS 12)

Readers of the Bible tend to take their task very seriously. After all, a long-standing emphasis among Wesleyan readers of Scripture is that a prayerful approach to Scripture opens them to the assistance or inspiration of the Holy Spirit, who will speak through those sacred words before them.[1] Thus persons approach the words of Scripture prayerfully and seriously because they anticipate God's Spirit to make those words and passages useful so that they are "equipped for every good work" (2 Tim. 3:17).

When reading narratives like Acts, the common assumption is that the episodes and characters will reflect the significance of the broader story of God at work among God's people. The beginning paragraph of Acts 12 conveys a solemn, serious period within the early decades of the Christian church. Although Luke offers little of the backstory, the mention of anyone named Herod (due to the family's history) would signify trouble for both God's purposes and the believers (cf. Luke 3:19-20; 9:7-9; 23:6-12). Herod's execution of the apostle

---

1. See, e.g., John Wesley's comment on 2 Timothy 3:16 in his *Explanatory Notes upon the New Testament* (London: Epworth, 1958), 794: "The Spirit of God not only once inspired those who wrote it, but continually inspires, supernaturally assists, those that read it with earnest prayer."

James was part of his larger program of arresting and persecuting those from the church (Acts 12:1-2). But the execution of James with the sword (probably by beheading), like crucifixion, was reserved for political threats and intended to shame the "culprit." Since the Lukan narrator notes that the popularity within Jewish circles of that murderous action led to Peter's arrest (vv. 3-5), the inference is that Peter's death might soon follow.

Yet amid such despair and weighty matters comes what is arguably the most comical episode in the New Testament. Luke the artistic storyteller may have been familiar with what was well known in broader Jewish and Greco-Roman contexts (not to mention contemporary times): that the comedic can teach serious lessons about history and life in general.[2] Such humor sometimes appears in the ways that narrators depict characters in episodes, especially minor characters and for Luke often at the expense of church leaders. But this means that readers of Acts must do more than merely recognize humorous aspects of the story when they appear; they should also consider how these function as parts of an episode and the larger narrative. Thus, in revisiting this familiar story, how might assessing the characterizations of Peter and Rhoda help readers to see a potential message that has been knocking at the door all along?

> **Luke the artistic storyteller may have been familiar with what was well known in broader Jewish and Greco-Roman contexts (not to mention contemporary times): that the comedic can teach serious lessons about history and life in general.**

The Characterization of Peter

Much of the characterization of Peter for Acts 12 depends on earlier narrative encounters with this character in Acts. For readers of Acts, Peter would be

---

2. See Kathy Chambers, "'Knock, Knock—Who's There?': Acts 12.6-17 as a Comedy of Errors," in *A Feminist Companion to the Acts of the Apostles*, ed. A.-J. Levine with M. Blickenstaff (Cleveland, OH: Pilgrim, 2004), 89.

perceived as a faithful leader among the apostles. He wisely guided the believers in the replacement of Judas as an apostle (1:15-26). He offered the explanation about Pentecost before skeptics (2:14-41). His involvement in the scandal with Ananias and Sapphira (5:1-11) depicts him not only as having divine insight but also as part of the believing community that was of "one heart and soul" (4:32, NRSVue), thereby caring for one another both economically and spiritually (see 2:42-47; 4:32-35). Peter was the apparent spokesperson before the Jewish council that arrested and harassed the apostles (5:17-42). And he was the recipient of a divine vision and then followed divine guidance to take the gospel message to the house of Cornelius (10:1-48), despite later facing questions and opposition from Jewish believers for such obedience (11:1-17). Thus, in the chapters leading up to Acts 12, Luke depicts Peter as a faithful Jewish leader and apostle among the believers who listened to the Spirit and obeyed God's guidance. So Peter's incarceration in Acts 12 once again placed him on the center stage of the narrative, since the political leader of that region singled him out as the leader of the earliest believers in an attempt to score some political points with the local people.

But Luke as the omniscient narrator offers an unusual description of Peter and his prison setting. He affords readers only a brief glance of the security arrangements (v. 6) to convince them that this prisoner could not possibly escape (as in a previous episode [5:17-42]).[3] Even Peter must have been convinced, since his deep sleep indicated that he was going nowhere. The angel's appearance before Peter and the accompanying light could not awaken him; only a hard punch to Peter's side from the angel could evoke a response from the slumbering apostle (12:7)![4] Even then, the angel needed to give the groggy,

---

3. See F. Scott Spencer, *Journeying through Acts: A Literary-Cultural Reading* (Peabody, MA: Hendrickson, 2004), 135: "Peter's notoriety for nocturnal jail-breaks has obviously preceded him!"

4. The verb *patassō*, which is often translated in more gentle terms as "tapped" (NRSVue) or "nudging" (CEB) in Acts 12:7, has stronger connotations for striking or punching someone (see NIV), as it is used later in verse 23.

confused Peter step-by-step instructions to get dressed and follow (vv. 8-9).[5] If readers would have any doubts, Luke gives some insight into what was going on inside Peter's head: his thought—that he was seeing a vision (v. 9)—was reminiscent of Peter's consternation over his heavenly vision at the house of Simon the tanner (cf. 10:9-16). Readers are thus given reason to hope that he, as before, would come around to understand what was happening. Not even the prison gate's opening by itself[6] helped Peter's befuddlement, since he seemingly sleepwalked out of prison with the angel without resistance (12:10). Only after the angel departed and Peter had walked at least a block from the prison did he come to his senses and recognize God's intervention on his behalf (vv. 10-11).

The Characterization of Rhoda

Unlike Peter, readers of Acts never encounter Rhoda anywhere in the narrative until Peter's release from prison and his decision to go to the house of Mary, the mother of John Mark, where others had gathered to pray (Acts 12:12).[7] When Peter knocked at the outer gate (which presumably opened into a small courtyard), Luke introduces Rhoda merely as a "female servant" (v. 13, CEB) who came to answer.[8] This simple introduction suggests two things: that Rhoda belonged to Mary, due to the location, and that Rhoda as a servant or slave was likely a stock character—known as a "running slave." This type of character

---

5. See Pervo, *Profit with Delight*, 62: "There is irony here, for Passover is the feast of liberation from bondage. Peter, held in bonds, will be freed. When the numinous glow fails to arouse the apostle, the angel tries a kick. . . . Like a patient parent, the angel must supervise his toilet. First the shoes are laced up, then his belt secured. Do not overlook the cloak. (All this will madden anxious readers. Why spend all this time perfecting the outfit? He is breaking out of jail, not going to a papal reception.)"

6. The Greek term *automatē* signifies how the gate opened on its own. From this term is derived the English word "automatic."

7. See Ivoni Richter Reimer, *Women in the Acts of the Apostles: A Feminist Liberation Perspective*, trans. L. M. Maloney (Minneapolis: Fortress, 1995), 241, who notes that this gathering of women for prayer on Peter's behalf relates to other positive images of the church that are associated with prayer.

8. The lack of a definite article preceding the term *paidiskē* suggests that Rhoda may have been one of multiple female slaves in this household (although the term may also refer to young girls).

typically functioned in several ways within Greco-Roman literature: "to intensify the anticipation of the reader, to develop irony (inasmuch as the reader has more knowledge of the situation than do the characters), and to provide comic relief at a critical juncture in the narrative when all seems lost."[9] Thus, despite her lower social status, the narrative spotlight illuminates Rhoda—rather than the recently released apostle at the gate—for all to notice in this brief moment.

Rhoda's response to Peter's knocking at the gate is the turning point of this episode. Interpreters often fixate on Rhoda's failure to open the gate as she joyfully announced Peter's presence to those in the house, thereby leaving Peter vulnerable on the street to soldiers looking for him (v. 14).[10] Note, however, that neither Luke nor anyone gathered in the house gives Rhoda a voice in this scene, since readers never hear what she reported. But readers *do* hear the response from those in the house, which not only *refuted* Rhoda's claim but *belittled* her, despite the fact that the good news she brought was supposedly the focus of their prayers (vv. 15-16). It was as though "they would rather believe that Peter is dead and so in the *inefficacy* of their prayer than heed the words of a female slave."[11]

Although the members of the prayer meeting refused to recognize the truth of Rhoda's claim, Rhoda herself had recognized Peter's presence *immediately*, not by seeing him at the gate, but merely by hearing his voice (v. 14). Yet readers themselves should also recognize the comical and absurd claim of the church members who countered Rhoda's insistence by saying, "It is his angel" (v. 15, NRSVue), since Luke had just told them about an angel who opened many doors and gates (and would not need to wait and knock at this one; see vv. 6-11). So like the women who were witnesses to Jesus's empty

---

9. See J. Albert Harrill, "The Dramatic Function of the Running Slave Rhoda (Acts 12.13-16): A Piece of Greco-Roman Comedy," *New Testament Studies* 46, no. 1 (2000): 151.

10. See, e.g., ibid., 156.

11. Chambers, "Knock, Knock," 94.

tomb and doggedly delivered the good news despite facing disbelief and ridicule (cf. Luke 24:1-12), this determined young female slave, who the Lukan narrator singles out, continued to stand as a witness to God's deliverance of Peter from near death, even though others around her had essentially taken away her voice.[12]

When the Knocking Stops . . .

According to Luke's account of the episode, the gathered church members never believed Rhoda's message. Yet Peter remained outside (perhaps in the cold) to fend for himself, continuing to knock at the outer gate that would lead him into the courtyard of Mary's house (Acts 12:16). How ironic that the iron gate of the prison could not secure Peter the prisoner *inside*, and yet the outer gate of Mary's house (and the disbelief of praying church members) kept him *outside*! The narrator mentions nothing specific that caused the group to open the gate, except for Peter's incessant knocking.[13] Perhaps they began to wonder, "So who's that knocking at the gate?" It is notable that those who downplayed the judgment and soundness of mind of a mere slave took on that same slave's role as a gatekeeper by opening the gate. And the omniscient narrator again provides some inside information not readily available to the average observer. In this instance, Luke shares the group's thoughts, stating that these who had been so quick to characterize Rhoda as someone who had lost her mind (v. 15) were "beside themselves" on discovering what Rhoda had revealed to them: that Peter really was at the gate (v. 16, AT).[14] But they only came to believe Rhoda's

---

12. See F. Scott Spencer, "Out of Mind, Out of Voice: Slave-Girls and Prophetic Daughters in Luke-Acts," *Biblical Interpretation* 7, no. 2 (April 1999): 144-45.

13. See Chambers, "Knock, Knock," 95, who suggests that Peter's knocking may also be a faint echo of Luke 18:1-8 (the parable of the persistent widow and the unjust judge).

14. The Greek verb *existēmi* is typically translated "astounded" (CEB), "astonished" (NIV), or "amazed" (NRSVue). However, the translation "beside oneself" conveys the word picture associated with the term's literal meaning (stand out of).

report after belatedly opening that gate for themselves.[15] So it may appear that Rhoda had the last laugh after all! At the same time, readers neither see Rhoda nor hear from her again in this episode.

The closing of the episode offers confirmation of Rhoda's claim about Peter's presence at the house. Interestingly, Luke never mentions whether the apostle entered Mary's house or just remained at the gate when he recounted his divine deliverance from prison (v. 17). Peter did not linger at the house, merely entrusting those gathered there to pass on the good news of his divine deliverance from prison to church leaders (v. 17). Although the narrator leaves open whether they did as Peter requested, the episode ends with the narrative attention again on Peter because of God's intervention. Despite the hopelessness that clouded the beginning of the chapter, the Lukan narrator assists readers of Acts (with some laughter thrown in) not only to see how God is still at work but also to anticipate what God might do next. And the unlikely character Rhoda helps readers not only to see these things but also to recognize that God may use unexpected persons as conduits of God's grace and guidance.

Conclusion

Although the ending of the episode reiterates that Peter had narrowly escaped Herod's deadly clutches because God rescued him, the following passage (Acts 12:20-24) reminds readers of a common Lukan theme: God has brought down the powerful and lifted up the lowly (see Luke 1:52). But that principle is not just about rulers in relation to the church. It also relates to different persons in the church, especially when they cannot "hear" another person's perspective about what God may be doing—a perspective that may be different from their own or even one that comes from someone different

---

15. See Spencer, "Out of Mind," 145.

from themselves in gender, status, ethnicity, and so on. This suggests that God may be at work among people and even in situations that we might least expect. But this also requires from us a willingness that allows God to make us aware—to open our eyes—so that we may perceive this divine activity around us.

Although persons may sometimes be quick to denounce whatever they dislike or whenever they disagree with someone or something, Rhoda's experience with the believers in Jerusalem reminds us, the church, of the importance of recognizing God's presence and grace in the unexpected places and people around us. And who knows? We might find evidence of God's deliverance and grace knocking at our door—even when we did not expect it! May it be so!

Questions for Consideration

1. What are some humorous or comedic scenes or episodes in the Bible that come to mind? How does humor contribute to the message of those passages?

2. What are some key aspects of the characterization of Peter that stand out for you in this episode? How do you see those descriptions contributing to the story?

3. What are some key aspects of the characterization of Rhoda that stand out for you in this episode? How do you see those descriptions contributing to the story?

4. Which of the characters in this episode—Peter, Rhoda, those gathered at the house—are most relatable for you? How does that character (or character group) help you understand this passage?

5. What may have caused those gathered at the house to downplay Rhoda's announcement about Peter? What may have been behind their suggestion that she was "out of [her] mind"?

6. What might be some reasons for Peter's quick exit from the house? What might these reasons suggest about the situation?

D. Repetition in Acts: Introduction

One of my favorite books on Acts is Richard I. Pervo's *Profit with Delight: The Literary Genre of the Acts of the Apostles* (Philadelphia: Fortress, 1987). I love the book, not because the author considers Acts to be historical fiction (which may be a controversial topic for some persons!), but because he highlights the creative and entertaining ways that the Lukan author composed this biblical work. And Pervo *himself* discusses these matters in rather entertaining ways. For instance, in considering the episode when Peter and the apostles were arrested in Jerusalem, appeared before the Jewish Sanhedrin, and were subsequently rescued by an angel in Acts 5, he writes,

> The Sanhedrin sits in solemn dignity, surrounded by the high priest and his entourage, all in all the "full senate of the children of Israel." With bated breath they await the proceedings that will extirpate this pernicious movement. Lackeys are dispatched to have the prisoners fetched, but there is a hitch. The accused are not in their cells. Benches creak. Tempers wear thin. Befuddled and terrified guards frantically seek the apostles, in fear for their lives (with reason: at 12:19 they will die). At last the escapees are located, in the temple, where they were previously seized. While the rulers of the nation sit in pompous arrogance, vexed over the time consumed by this tawdry affair, the followers of Jesus are doing the job of their accusers: teaching the people. Brave apostles make the Sanhedrin look both wicked and foolish.[1]

---

1. Pervo, *Profit with Delight*, 61-62.

Pervo argues throughout his work that the Lukan author uses a variety of literary devices—wit and humor, irony, burlesque and rowdy episodes (which provoke "scornful laughter at what is ugly or unusual, at the misfortunes of others, or at raucous violence"[2]), and visions, just to name several—to accomplish his purposes in the book of Acts. The author realizes that he not only has a story to tell but also needs to tell that story well to maintain the attention and interest of the audience. Thus the author was well skilled in appropriating literary devices that would help make the story come alive in ways that would convey what he hoped.

Interestingly, two of what might be considered the most dramatic episodes of Acts—the episode in Acts 9 of the risen Jesus's confrontation with Saul, the persecutor of the believers, and the episode in Acts 10 of the divine callings and subsequent meeting of the Gentile Cornelius and the apostle Peter in Caesarea Philippi—receive only scant attention and treatment in Pervo's work.

> **Although repetition or redundancy may initially appear to be unnecessary and may create an illusion of wordiness, its most common function in ancient literature was clarification and emphasis.**

It is doubtful that Pervo failed to recognize the dramatic aspects of these two significant scenes near the heart of the Acts narrative. But perhaps Pervo was captivated by more entertaining literary devices such as irony, wit and humor, suspense, and danger and downplayed more subtle literary devices such as repetition (also known as redundancy). Although repetition or redundancy may initially appear to be unnecessary and may create an illusion of wordiness, its most common function in ancient literature was clarification and emphasis.[3]

When writers used manual typewriters to prepare documents, there was no formal mechanism for boldface fonts. However, typists developed an informal

---

2. Ibid., 61.
3. See the important chapter on repetition in Meir Sternberg, *The Poetics of Biblical Narrative: Ideological Literature and the Drama of Reading* (Bloomington, IN: Indiana University Press, 1985), 365–440, esp. 368.

way to type a word in bold print: type the word the first time, then backspace to the beginning of the word and retype the same word in the same space a second time, and finally repeat that process a third time. The *repetition* of typing the same word *several* times created what was essentially a boldface font, and that repetition emphasized or highlighted that word. Similarly, repetition within a narrative (or any other literary form, for that matter) results in some form of emphasis or clarification through emphasis.

Repetition or redundancy may take different forms. For instance, words or ideas may be repeated. But repetition or redundancy may occur in many other ways, such as the expansion or reduction of a story, changes to the story's order when it is retold, rewording of the story, or the substitution of a different description for a key element of the story.[4] In the cases of Saul's encounter with the risen Jesus or the meeting of Cornelius and Peter in Acts, these scenes are also repeated in Acts three times! Such repetition suggests the importance of these scenes within the Acts narrative. At the same time, with the repetition may come different ways of telling these stories, so with shared emphases come some differences that also contribute to the narrative. A close reading of these episodes side by side has the potential of highlighting both similarities and differences that may work together in reading through the book of Acts.

---

4. Ibid., 391-92.

8

Saul's/Paul's Encounter with Jesus . . . in Triplicate

(ACTS 9, 22, 26)

One of the most memorable Lukan stories in Acts is about the confrontation between the risen Jesus and Saul, the persecutor of the believers. In this episode we have numerous dramatic elements: the shocking encounter out of nowhere, the startling voice of Jesus, the blindness that renders the powerful Saul dependent on the help of others, and an additional divine encounter with a fearful and questioning disciple, just to name a few. There are also many things that Luke does not mention. For instance, nothing is stated about the reasons behind Saul's opposition to the Jesus followers.[1] However, that confrontation by the resurrected Jesus on that road to Damascus radically changed everything for both Saul and the earliest believers, since the persecutor and enemy of the early Jesus movement became the one who *himself* was persecuted and imprisoned for his proclamation of the Christian message.

Although Acts depicts numerous instances of divine intervention, particularly those with believers in prison (see, e.g., Acts 5, 12, and 16), one may contend that this specific encounter in Acts 9 stands as one of the most significant

---

1. I have hypothesized that clues of Saul's opposition may be found in Paul's letters, especially 1–2 Corinthians. For instance, 1 Corinthians 1:18-25 describes the idea of a crucified Christ as foolishness and weakness, as well as a "stumbling block" to Jews (v. 23). In addition, Paul admitted in 2 Corinthians 5:16 that "even though we once knew Christ from a human point of view, we no longer know him in that way" (NRSVue). These comments suggest that the persecutor Saul saw the idea of a dead Christ/Messiah by way of the humiliating Roman death of crucifixion as nothing less than an impossibility—an oxymoron.

instances of divine intervention in the entire Acts narrative. To be sure, what happened here set the stage for the reemergence of Saul (later Paul) in Acts 11, who would then become the major (human) character of the narrative from Acts 13 on. Yet the importance of what happened seems to be underscored by the fact that descriptions of this scene appear *three* times, not only in Acts 9 but also in Acts 22 and 26 (9:1-19*a*; 22:4-16; 26:12-18). The repetition alone suggests how pivotal this divine encounter was to almost everything else that happened subsequently in Acts.

However, with the repetition of the story come both similarities in how the story is told as well as different narrations of this story. On the one hand, those similarities will likely point to emphases that the versions of the story share. On the other hand, those differences will *also* contribute to the Acts narrative but through those differences (rather than through similarities and emphases). The fact that this first account alone comes from the perspective of the Lukan narrator (unlike the other two, which are placed on the lips of Paul) suggests that one may discover distinctive Lukan themes that will appear later in Acts. But readers of Acts should anticipate all three versions contributing to the Lukan perspective reflected by the Acts narrative.

Reading the Three Versions of Saul's Encounter with the Risen Jesus

Because the three accounts of Saul's encounter with the risen Jesus appear in different sections of the Acts narrative, readers of Acts must interpret each of them according to its context and placement within that narrative. This allows readers to assess both *how* the narrator tells the story and *why* the narrator has shaped the story for that literary setting.

1. Acts 9:1-19*a*

The first account appears within the Acts context where the church and its witness about the resurrection of Jesus spread beyond Jerusalem to other "peoples," beginning with Judea and Samaria (Acts 8:4–12:25; cf. 1:8). Most of the attention in these chapters is given to groups and individuals who would have been considered either outsiders or on the margins from a Jewish perspective. Although the religious status of such persons may have been in question, the extension of the gospel message to them indicated that God's call of salvation and membership within the people of God also included them. So questionable Samaritans (whom the Jewish people historically despised [8:5-25]), an Ethiopian eunuch (who would have been considered unworthy to enter the temple in Jerusalem for worship [vv. 26-40]), and even Gentiles (who had not converted to Judaism [10:1-48]) were welcomed. And the Lukan narrator tells of their diverse "conversion" stories[2] or at least offers these different stories of transformation as a result of the Christian message.

Luke's placement of Saul's encounter with the risen Jesus within a series of conversion stories suggests that readers should also engage this story from a similar perspective. Religious zeal drove Saul's harassment and pursuit of the believers (see 9:1-2). What stopped him was a light from heaven that caused him to fall to the ground, where he was questioned, "Saul, Saul, why do you persecute me?" (v. 4). His response—"Who are you, Lord?" (v. 5)—probably is an address of respect, "Sir." But the irony is obvious, as Saul correctly identified the speaker and validated the gospel that he vehemently opposed!

After the risen Jesus identified himself, he instructed Saul to get up and enter the city, where he would be told what he must do (v. 6). But because he was blinded by the light, Saul was led by the hand into Damascus, where he stayed for three days. It was only after a reluctant disciple named Ananias (see vv. 10-14)—to whom the risen Jesus also appeared and informed about Saul's

---

2. The diversity of these stories and "conversion experiences" would also imply that readers of Acts should be open to what the word "conversion" might mean within the narrative. Conversion may broadly involve changes in life and perspective, notably for what God has done through Jesus. Since, in all these instances, there may have already been some belief in the one and only God of Israel, "conversion" may not refer to changing their beliefs in God but changing some of their beliefs about God and what God is doing. Thus the narrator of Acts may encourage readers of Acts to see "conversion" in a lot of different persons and places, since God's movement into "all the world" challenged common assumptions about God and God's purposes. And it still does!

divine calling or commission to *both* Jews and Gentiles (vv. 15-16)—met with Saul that he was healed and baptized (vv. 17-18), a sign of his inclusion within the church and the people of God. It was not long before Saul began preaching about Jesus in the synagogues of Damascus, the same place where he planned to arrest those who affirmed such preaching (vv. 20-21).

Thus three elements of this episode stand out most prominently: *(a)* the *divine confrontation* of Saul by the risen Jesus (vv. 3-6), *(b)* the *divine call or commission* of Saul as explained to Ananias (vv. 15-16), and *(c)* the *divine healing* of Saul through the agent Ananias (vv. 17-18). What is most surprising about the second element is that this so-called commission was spoken only to Ananias, and nowhere in this episode does the Lukan narrative explicitly mention Saul receiving it. Yet the Lord's words describing his divine calling—that he was "my chosen instrument to proclaim my name to the Gentiles and their kings and to the people of Israel" (v. 15)—stands out as a concise explanatory statement for understanding the ministry of the one later called Paul. And the Lukan narrator teases readers of Acts to imagine that divine calling in the meeting between Ananias and Saul, when Ananias explained that he had come so that Saul might "see again and be filled with the Holy Spirit" (v. 17), the latter descriptor being a common feature of those in Acts who served and proclaimed the gospel message.

2. Acts 22:4-16

The second account of Saul's encounter with the risen Jesus appears in a very different context within Acts. Paul (formerly Saul) had returned to Jerusalem after ministering throughout the eastern Mediterranean region (see Acts 16–20). In response to some accusations from Jerusalem church leaders about his teaching, Paul had spent nearly a week as a participant in a Jewish purification ritual at the temple in Jerusalem (21:18-24). Due to other Jewish accusers who saw Paul there but also assumed that he brought a non-Jewish person into the temple (vv. 27-29), a riot quickly escalated that endangered Paul's life (vv. 30-32). Despite Paul's apparent innocence, his arrest by Roman officials (probably for inciting the riot) spared his life (vv. 33-34). The crowd's persistence in calling for Paul's execution (note their chants—"Away with him!"—in v. 36 [NRSVue]) is reminiscent of an earlier crowd's cries against Jesus (see Luke 23:18). So after Paul requested permission to address them, his context is not a third-person narrative, as in Acts 9, but a first-person defense (see 22:1).

The initial story outlined in Paul's defense is similar to the Lukan version of Acts 9. The opening portion highlights Paul's background as a faithful, pious person of the Jewish faith. The general account of the encounter on the road to Damascus echoes the first account. The major difference in this account is that those with Saul did not hear the voice speaking with Saul (22:9; cf. 9:7), with that voice also indicating that Saul would be told everything that he had been "assigned to do" (22:10). The different audience may be the reason for this varied account, since it would imply that the message was intended only for Saul.

The role of Ananias is much different in the second version. Whereas Ananias was a reluctant participant in the first account, Paul's version depicts him as a well-respected person within the Jewish community who came to Paul and restored his sight (vv. 12-13). Unlike the first account, Ananias pronounced God's commission over Saul by declaring that he would be God's "witness to all people" about what he had "seen and heard" (v. 15). Thus, in this second account, the commission or calling of Saul is accentuated. Although the healing (from blindness) is present, that calling seems to be the climax of this version of the story.

3. Acts 26:12-18

The third version of Saul's encounter with the risen Jesus also has a unique literary context. After his arrest in Jerusalem, Paul (formerly Saul) remained in custody for the remainder of Acts. That custody was affected by threats on his life (see Acts 23:12-22) and official corruption (see 24:24-27), which prompted his appeal to Caesar (25:1-12). Despite such issues, Paul was granted an official hearing before Festus and King Agrippa for purposes of preparing the legal documents that would accompany Paul to Rome.

In many respects, the third version of Saul's encounter with the risen Jesus is a condensed version of the first two. There is no mention of Ananias, nor is there any mention of Saul's blindness or any subsequent healing. Everything that happened occurred during that brief encounter on the road—not later as they appear in Acts 9 and 22. What is most significant is that the Lord himself, not Ananias, commissioned Paul (26:16-18). This leaves the reader to contemplate what Paul mentions last in the episode: his divine commission. This commission includes both a promise ("I will rescue you from your own people and from the Gentiles" [v. 17]) and also a distinct mission ("I am sending you to them to open their eyes and turn them from darkness to light" [vv. 17-18]). Not only does this emphasis contribute to the literary setting (i.e., Paul's hearing before the Roman officials), it also underscores what has been lacking for the readers of Acts in the previous versions: the precise or direct commission or calling that the Lord spoke to Paul.[3]

Assessing the Repeated Accounts of Saul's Encounter with the Risen Jesus in Acts

When reading a narrative like Acts, there is little doubt that its readers should account for materials as they appear sequentially within the narrative. After all, narratives are meant to be read from beginning to end. So when readers discover repeated materials or episodes like Saul's encounter with the risen Jesus in chapters 9, 22, and 26, they should account for the presence and form of each account as each appears within its place and context in Acts.

---

3. See Charles W. Hedrick, "Paul's Conversion/Call: A Comparative Analysis of the Three Reports in Acts," *Journal of Biblical Literature* 100, no. 3 (September 1981): 427.

But ancient (and contemporary) authors used repetition (or redundancy) to emphasize and clarify significant ideas and perspectives within a narrative. Such literary repetition helps the narrator to hammer home matters of importance. But in the case of episodes like Saul's encounter, repetition rarely appears as mere verbatim recitation or copying of one version into another context. Here in Acts, different versions appear in different contexts with different emphases.

So how does this type of repetition influence readers of Acts? Interpreters of Acts have long wrestled with the question of what type of story these episodes might be. That is, are these conversion stories? Or commission/call stories? Or miracle/healing stories? And the reason for raising such questions is that a particular way of reading accompanies each type of story (just as someone reads a murder mystery differently from a romance novel or a biography). But some of these episodes contain characteristics of multiple types of stories. So how does someone account for these features among these similar episodes?

When interpreting these three accounts of Saul's encounter with the risen Jesus, readers of Acts should consider three things. First, context matters. Each episode has a unique context that informs how one should read and interpret it. But one should not assume that the context that defines one account also defines and informs the others. For instance, the first account has a distinct context involving conversion and transformation, especially for persons and individuals associated with God and God's people. Thus the possibility of seeing the account in Acts 9 within broader conversations of conversion (and perhaps understanding the episode to be about the conversion of Saul) is certainly plausible.[4] But the carryover of that emphasis to the corresponding episodes of Acts 22 and 26, as is often seen in Bible section titles, may not adequately consider differences of context for these different versions.

---

4. One could also contend that the Acts 9 account is a healing or miracle story, given the prominence of Ananias and his role in the healing of Saul's blindness. However, that would not be the case in Acts 26, where neither Ananias nor Saul's blindness are mentioned.

Second, note elements of the story that drop out as the episode is told and retold within Acts. Two aspects of the story that diminish are noteworthy. One is the character Ananias. As Saul's role increases (which is not surprising, given who tells the story the last two times!), Ananias's place first decreases and then disappears.[5] And corresponding with that is the role of Saul's blindness. In Acts 9, the one who was blind for three days (v. 9) was later healed as "something like scales" dramatically fell from Saul's eyes (v. 18). But in Acts 22, the description is toned down, with the wording suggesting that Saul simply could not see due to the bright light (v. 11) and that Ananias merely spoke and Saul's sight later returned (v. 13). However, in Acts 26 there is no mention of Saul's loss of sight whatsoever. Instead, there are references to what Saul and others can see as a result of his calling:

> Now get up and stand on your feet. *I have appeared to you* to appoint you as a servant and *as a witness of what you have seen and will see of me.* I will rescue you from your own people and from the Gentiles. I am sending you to them *to open their eyes* and turn them from darkness to light, and from the power of Satan to God, so that they may receive forgiveness of sins and a place among those who are sanctified by faith in me. (Vv. 16-18, emphasis added)[6]

Thus one may contend that the references to blindness on Saul's part have been dropped. However, the references to blindness have been replaced by images of seeing in connection with Paul's divine calling.

Third, be prepared to explain the presence of additional details or materials that suddenly appear or gain prominence in the narrative. Despite the gradual reduction that seems to occur in the telling of this episode, there is one drastic change or addition in the version of Acts 26. Up to this point, the Lukan

---

5. See Ronald D. Witherup, "Functional Redundancy in the Acts of the Apostles: A Case Study," *Journal for the Study of the New Testament* 48 (1992): 73-74.

6. See Dennis Hamm, "Paul's Blindness and Its Healing: Clues to Symbolic Intent (Acts 9; 22 and 26)," *Biblica* 71, no. 1 (1990): 66-67.

narrator had given readers access to Saul's divine commission in indirect or secondhand ways. In Acts 9, readers gained access to the substance of Saul's commission by "overhearing" the risen Jesus's explanation to Ananias about what Saul's ministry would entail (see vv. 15-16). And in Acts 22, the account details Ananias's words of commissioning to Saul after restoring his sight (see vv. 14-15). Thus, in the first two versions, the nature of Saul's commissioning was recounted by Jesus or Ananias. That is, in neither account do readers see or hear Saul *himself* commissioned or called by God (although one may still affirm such a commission as divine in nature). But in the last version, in Acts 26, Saul ends the account by describing that commissioning as spoken by the Lord on the Damascus road. And that is why he could affirm before King Agrippa, "I wasn't disobedient to that heavenly vision" (v. 19, CEB). As a result, this last account may well be a commission/call story, even if the first one is not. But readers of Acts may only come to conclusions like this by recognizing the features of repetition in the book of Acts.

Questions for Consideration

1. What are some basic features of repetition (or redundancy) that might be part of Acts or other biblical books?

2. What do you see as similarities between the three passages that describe Saul's encounter with the risen Jesus (Acts 9:1-19*a*; 22:4-16; 26:12-18)?

3. What are repeated or redundant features of Acts 9:1-19*a* in relation to Acts 22:4-16? Or Acts 26:12-18?

4. In what way(s) might these passages relate to one another or build upon one another? Explain.

5. What kind of story do you understand each of these passages to be? Commission/calling? Healing? Conversion? Explain.

9

Cornelius and Peter, Told Over and Over Again

(ACTS 10-11, 15)

For centuries, the incident in Acts 10 where Peter travels to the home of the Gentile Cornelius and proclaims the Christian gospel has been interpreted as significant to Acts. The extended episode may recount the first presentation of the gospel message to a non-Jewish audience. However, in more recent years a good number of scholars have argued that this extended episode is the *second*, not the first, instance of Gentile acceptance of the good news. The reason for this reinterpretation is the recognition that the Ethiopian eunuch in Acts 8, whom Philip encounters in the unlikely place of a road in the desert between Jerusalem and Gaza (on the Mediterranean coast, southwest of Jerusalem), would not have been considered Jewish, given his physical condition as a eunuch.[1] If this reinterpretation is valid, then one must look for other clues to why this episode was included within Acts.

Two other characteristics of this extended episode suggest something about its importance that should not be ignored. First, the entire description of all that occurs encompasses the entirety of Acts 10. Although that may not seem all that important, no other episode in Acts receives as much attention as this one does. This alone suggests that there must be some reasons for the inclusion

---

1. See chapter 6 of this book. The major question concerning this understanding of the Ethiopian eunuch has to do with the narrator's comment that the eunuch was returning home from Jerusalem, where he had gone to worship (Acts 8:27-28). This note is puzzling, since eunuchs were not allowed into the temple for worship.

of this episode and the attention it receives. Second, the repetition about this incident insinuates that there are significant aspects of this story that the reader of Acts must keep in mind. Considering that repeated elements may be found both within the narrated episode itself and then later in Acts 11 and 15, it is plausible to surmise from this evidence that there is something critically important to the narrative of Acts that the reader must discover.

The questions about the events in Cornelius's house that arose in the minds both of those who accompanied Peter (Acts 10:45-46) and of those in the Jerusalem church (11:1-2) suggest that these occurrences were more problematic than what our own minds as contemporary readers may be able to grasp initially. Interestingly, although the Lukan narrator interjects no direct references to the Jewish Scriptures in these episodes, what every telling and retelling seem to imply is that something had happened that *contradicted* the traditional Jewish interpretation of those Scriptures. That is, unlike Peter's speeches on the day of Pentecost (2:14-41) or in the temple after the healing of the lame man (3:11-26), there is nothing in his message at the house of Cornelius (10:34-43) or later in his explanation to the Jerusalem church (11:5-17) that interprets this episode on the basis of Scripture. It is no wonder that this episode makes such a mess of things! Yet here it stands, with all its unanswered questions. And it is repeated again and again!

It would have been nice if the Lukan author had decided to include one of his characteristic summary statements here in this chapter so that readers would not be left wondering about what is going on here. After all, if the Jewish Scriptures offer little help, we really do not have much upon which to build an interpretive case. Yet perhaps the author of Acts is doing what the ancient writer Demetrius mentions in his work *On Style*:

> Not all points should be punctiliously and tediously elaborated, but some should be left to the comprehension and inference of the hearer, who when he perceives what you have left unsaid becomes not only your hearer but

[also] your witness, and a very friendly witness too. For he thinks himself intelligent because you have afforded him the means of showing his intelligence. It seems like a slur on your hearer to tell him everything as though he were a simpleton. (4.222)

The Lukan author thus may have left readers without an explanation because, like the repeated references back to this episode, everything readers need to make valid conclusions is right there before them. And it is in the process of discovery, rather than in an explanation, that we truly hear the voice of God.

Unlike the three accounts of Saul's encounter with the risen Jesus (Acts 9, 22, 26), the repeated accounts of the story of Cornelius and Peter include greater variations among them, with the first account being more detailed and subsequent versions more abbreviated. Thus attention here will focus first on selected Lukan emphases that are repeated in those accounts: the characterization of Cornelius and Peter, the depictions of their visions, and the descriptions of the divine response toward the Gentile audience at Cornelius's house.

The Characterization of Cornelius and Peter

As has already been established in this book, the narrator of Acts sets up a character both by direct description of the person and through that person's actions. The initial description of Cornelius that Luke offers is mostly positive. His position as a centurion within the Italian cohort (Acts 10:1) would indicate that Cornelius was non-Jewish and thus unable to observe Torah.[2] However, he would have enjoyed significant social and financial standing within society. How Luke depicts Cornelius is consistent with pious Jewish persons of that era: a devout person (v. 2), a generous giver of offerings on behalf of the needy within the Jewish community (v. 2), and someone who constantly prayed to

---

2. See Beverly Roberts Gaventa, *From Darkness to Light: Aspects of Conversion in the New Testament*, Overtures to Biblical Theology 20 (Philadelphia: Fortress, 1986), 112.

God (v. 2). That Luke portrays him as a person who feared God (v. 2) likely identifies him as a Gentile who was attracted to Jewish worship, faith, and practices and who probably attended the Jewish synagogue but who had not become a circumcised Jewish proselyte.[3] That this characterization of Cornelius was substantively repeated by his representatives who were sent to Peter (see v. 22) underscores the significance of his piety, especially since he was a Gentile.

Cornelius also stood out in comparison to some of the other characters who had appeared in the last couple of chapters in Acts. Unlike the Ethiopian eunuch, there is no indication that Cornelius was having difficulties understanding the Jewish Scriptures (8:26-40). And unlike Saul, Cornelius had not been a persecutor of the church (vv. 1-3; 9:1-2). So whatever Cornelius might need, it was not a radical transformation from a life of overt sinfulness.

Unlike Cornelius, Luke's depiction of Peter relies on Peter's prominence within the Acts narrative.[4] His reputation as a faithful apostle and leader of the church precedes him through the previous nine chapters of Acts. Readers can see Peter's role within the church in the request for him to come following the death of Dorcas (9:36-41). But what may be most notable is the place where Paul was temporarily staying in Joppa when the representatives from Cornelius summoned him: the house of Simon the tanner (v. 43). Not only was the city's population mostly Gentile, but Simon's profession as a tanner was notorious for its unpleasant stench and its perpetual "unclean" status within Jewish circles due to the tanner's work with dead animals, animal blood, and urine used in the tanning process. Peter's housing arrangements with a man of questionable status prior to landing in Caesarea may have prepared him for what he encountered there.[5] That this was not repeated in subsequent retellings of this story suggests that this information may have been more helpful (and potentially less

---

3. See Irina Levinskaya, *The Book of Acts in Its Diaspora Setting*, The Book of Acts in Its First Century Setting 5 (Grand Rapids: Eerdmans, 1996), 51-126, and Joseph B. Tyson, "Jews and Judaism in Luke-Acts: Reading as a Godfearer," *New Testament Studies* 41 (1995): 19-38.

4. See chapter 7 of this book.

5. See Thompson, *Acts*, 202.

problematic) for the readers of Acts than for the believers in Jerusalem!

As the narrator introduces these two men in Acts 10, the only relationship between them is that they both were pious and seemingly intent on doing God's will. Nothing suggests a personal acquaintance between them, with just over thirty miles separating their locations. But these aspects become less important in subsequent accounts, since the narrator seems to assume that readers understand these basic aspects about the two key characters.

The Depictions of the Visions of Cornelius and Peter

What is remarkable in this episode is that divine visions came to both men. The visions themselves are seemingly unrelated. In both cases, the visions appeared while the men were apparently in prayer (see Acts 10:3, 9), which suggests both divine favor and guidance.[6] On the one hand, the four accounts of Cornelius's vision reiterate God's initiative and Cornelius's obedience to that vision (vv. 1-8, 22, 30-33; 11:11-14). The divine initiative is accentuated because an angel appeared and spoke to Cornelius through this vision—the only instance in Acts when a Gentile was the recipient of an angelic visitation (10:3, 22, 30).[7] The angel not only confirmed Cornelius's pious practices before God but gave him instructions about summoning Peter (vv. 5, 22, 31-32; 11:13-14). The first account mentions no reason for summoning Peter (just do it), but the latter three versions indicate that Peter had a message for them (but the essence of that message was undisclosed).[8] Finally, in Luke's narration of the initial vision and Cornelius's later recollection of that same

---

6. The common interpretation of the timing of Cornelius's vision (at three in the afternoon) is that Cornelius was praying because it was a Jewish hour of prayer, which Cornelius himself later reiterated (Acts 10:30). See, e.g., Luke Timothy Johnson, *The Acts of the Apostles*, Sacra Pagina Series 5 (Collegeville, MN: Liturgical, 1992), 182, and Spencer, *Journeying through Acts*, 119.

7. See Beverly Roberts Gaventa, *The Acts of the Apostles*, Abingdon New Testament Commentaries (Nashville: Abingdon, 2003), 164.

8. See Ronald D. Witherup, "Cornelius Over and Over and Over Again: 'Functional Redundancy' in the Acts of the Apostles," *Journal for the Study of the New Testament* 49 (1993): 56, who notes that Cornelius's account of his vision adds Cornelius's comment to Peter (Acts 10:33), which sets up Peter's speech (vv. 34-43). Thus Cornelius's role begins to diminish within the Acts narrative.

vision, Cornelius's immediate response was one of obedience: he promptly sent for Peter as instructed (10:7-8, 22, 33; 11:13-14). In Peter's report to the Jerusalem believers, his summary of Cornelius's vision—which was in response to their criticism that he had entered "the home of the uncircumcised" (CEB) and shared a meal with them (11:3)—emphasized God's guidance through the angel (vv. 13-14).[9]

On the other hand, the accounts of Peter's vision may describe a different message conveyed to Peter but also focus on related issues in Cornelius's vision so readers may compare them. In contrast to the vision of Cornelius, Luke narrates Peter's vision only twice (10:9-16; 11:5-10). However, within Peter's vision there is an assertion that the vision occurred "three times" (10:16; 11:10), which may reiterate its significance. Peter's vision included no sighting of God or an angel, but his vision included a voice from heaven (10:13, 15), which he did not mention to Cornelius but later revealed during his interrogation before the Jerusalem believers (11:9). Both the heavenly voice and the sheet with the animals, reptiles, and birds coming down from heaven are suggestive of the vision's divine source. And Peter's response—"Lord!"—to the voice (10:14) indicates his recognition of God's message and guidance.

However, unlike the Gentile Cornelius, Peter initially resisted the divine instruction, not just saying no but using a strong negative to indicate that he had *never* eaten anything common or unclean (v. 14). Interestingly, in Peter's recounting of this vision to the Jerusalem believers in Acts 11, the objection was slightly different: that nothing common or unclean had entered his mouth (v. 8). The first version emphasizes Peter's own adherence to food regulations, while the second version accentuates a general understanding of commonness and uncleanness. The latter version moved beyond what one eats to how one views all reality, animal and human alike, which God has deemed "clean" and

---

9. See ibid., 57, which notes that Cornelius's role is clearly secondary to the larger message, since Cornelius is not described by his piety and is not even named.

therefore where God may be at work.[10] Although the divine vision initially confused Peter and prompted his resistance, his act of witness before Cornelius and others was a sign of his evolving understanding (see 10:34, "I now realize . . .") of God's work among the Gentiles. And with that, Cornelius himself would fade into the narrative background of Acts.

It should be noted that the brief account of Acts 15 mentions nothing about any divine vision to Peter. But Peter's declaration before the gathering of the Jerusalem Council—that "God chose me from among you as the one through whom the Gentiles would hear the word of the gospel and come to believe" (v. 7, CEB)—alludes to this vision, along with God's guidance that led to Peter's proclamation of the gospel message to the gathered Gentiles at Cornelius's house. But by merely alluding to the vision, the Lukan narrator keeps the focus on God (who orchestrated the meeting) and on the significance of the story: the divine occurrence among the gathered Gentiles.[11]

The Descriptions of the Divine Response toward the Gentile Audience at Cornelius's House

The Lukan description of God's response toward the Gentiles who had gathered at Cornelius's house is significant in the initial version of the story and in both of Peter's recountings of that meeting. In Acts 10, Luke depicts Peter delivering a short speech or message about Jesus before the receptive audience of Gentiles who had come with anticipation to hear what he might say (cf. vv. 30-33). But Peter's message was interrupted, not by persons uncomfortable with what was happening (although the circumcised believers who accompanied Peter must have been fidgeting in their seats over what was occurring; cf. v. 45), but by the Holy Spirit coming upon the audience.[12]

---

10. See ibid., 59.

11. See ibid., 61.

12. See Joshua D. Garroway, "'Apostolic Irresistibility' and the Interrupted Speeches in Acts," *Catholic Biblical Quarterly* 74, no. 4 (2012): 751.

According to the narrator, what made it clear to Peter and the other Jewish believers with him that this was a genuine outpouring of the Spirit was that it resembled what happened on the day of Pentecost in Jerusalem (10:46; cf. 2:1-4). However, the recipients of the gift of the Holy Spirit in Cornelius's house were not *Jewish* but *Gentile*. This could explain why the circumcised believers who were also present at the meeting were not merely astonished but "beside themselves" over these Gentiles receiving the Spirit (10:45, AT).[13] Peter's rhetorical question about who might withhold baptism from these Gentiles (v. 47; cf. 8:36) may have anticipated a negative response from these Jewish companions, since it forced everyone to acknowledge God's intervention in the meeting and blessing on the Gentiles.[14]

Peter's recounting of the event to the group of criticizing Jewish believers in Acts 11 also reiterates the coming of the Spirit upon the Gentiles who had gathered. He repeated twice what the initial version emphasized: that the coming of the Spirit was similar ("the same gift"; v. 17) to what the Jewish believers experienced earlier (vv. 15, 17), presumably at Pentecost (cf. 2:1-4). Three differences stand out. First, Peter did not describe the coming of the Spirit as happening after he had been speaking for a while but when he first began to speak (11:15). This places the emphasis on God's initiative, not Peter's eloquent message. Second, Peter linked what happened to Jesus's promise: "You will be baptized with the Holy Spirit" (see 1:5). Third, Peter acknowledged that God, not he, was responsible for all that happened at Cornelius's house, since he was unable (and unwilling) to stand in God's way.[15] Such evidence led to the recognition of what God had done.

---

13. Note that Luke uses the same verb (*existēmi*) to describe the response of the circumcised believers to the Gentiles' receiving the Spirit at Cornelius's house (Acts 10:45) and the response of the gathered believers at Mary's house at the discovery of Peter at the gate (12:16). See chapter 7 in this book.

14. See Garroway, "Apostolic Irresistibility," 751, who suggests that the Jewish believers who accompanied Peter may have been responsible for some bickering about his response to Cornelius, so "a miraculous intervention secures acquiescence from everyone."

15. The verb used here (Acts 15:17) to refer to standing in God's way (*kōlyō*) is also used in a rhetorical question to refer to hindering the Ethiopian eunuch (8:36—see chapter 6 of this book) and the Gentiles at Cornelius's house (10:47) from being baptized. In all three instances, the emphasis is on the absence of such hindrance.

The last and shortest version, found in Acts 15, does not mention Cornelius or the visions of Cornelius or Peter. Peter's retelling to the apostles and elders at Jerusalem mostly emphasizes God's role in the meeting at Cornelius's house. Although the Gentiles heard the gospel message through Peter, Peter underscores these things about God: (1) *God chose* him as God's instrument (v. 7), (2) *God* testified to the Gentiles by giving them the Holy Spirit (v. 8), and (3) *God* made no distinction between the Jews and Gentiles by cleansing the hearts of the Gentiles by faith (v. 9). That is, God was the main mover and actor at Cornelius's house, not Peter. Since God was responsible for the Gentiles' salvation, Peter emphasized that this was nothing that the Jewish believers did not know, since the salvation of all persons—Jewish and Gentile alike—comes "through the grace of the Lord Jesus" (v. 11, NRSVue). That is, all are dependent on what God has done through Christ.

Repeating the Story of Cornelius and Peter in Acts

Sometimes, contemporary readers question the place of repetition in a literary work. Concern for information over literary effect often leads to a desire for authors to "get to the point" rather than use elaboration or redundancy to underscore something. Yet for ancient authors, repetition was a common means of communicating significant themes or ideas within a work, and alterations to different versions of an episode enhanced the author's ability to highlight and accentuate matters of importance.

For the narrative of Acts, the emphases on divine initiative and obedience concerning the events at Cornelius's house were significant for the earliest believers wrestling with the legitimacy of what took place. Because Jewish purity laws and systems clarified how persons related to a holy God and an unholy world, readers should not be surprised that Peter was criticized for what seemed to be rogue behavior by going to a gathering at a Gentile's house (not to mention staying for a few days, as 10:48 notes in passing). Even leaders like Peter would not "get a pass" on something that seemed to violate every basic rule in the book.

But biblical narratives are more than just stories to read for information. In addition to offering episodes that tease readers to think differently and propose different perspectives about God, the world, and the church, narratives also nudge us in particular ways. And one way that they prod us along is by helping us to see things by repeating them over and over again. This is because it may not be enough for us merely to see biblical passages affirming God's grace extending to others beyond our "holy group." Rather, it is quite another matter to witness the call of God on others—both through instant obedience and even after initial resistance—to be conduits of God's grace to persons and groups who have been deemed "outsiders": those considered outside of the realm of God's grace and therefore unworthy of being embraced or even considered as part of the people of God.

> For ancient authors, repetition was a common means of communicating significant themes or ideas within a work, and alterations to different versions of an episode enhanced the author's ability to highlight and accentuate matters of importance.

What these versions of the story of Cornelius and Peter remind us is that Cornelius may not have been the person who most needed conversion. On the one hand, one could argue that Cornelius had not yet heard the message about Jesus, so this story is ultimately about his conversion. But his life was much like the Jewish believers prior to Pentecost. On the other hand, Peter also needed conversion, as his response to the divine vision revealed. But because he was open to God's guidance and correction, he was able to recognize the Spirit's movement upon the Gentiles at Cornelius's house and recall Jesus's promise about the baptism with the Spirit.[16] Yet still others, the Jewish believers—who

---

16. See Gaventa, *From Darkness to Light*, 112-21.

accompanied Peter to Cornelius's house and others who criticized him for what happened there—also needed conversion, but seemed more resistant to God's leading.[17] Their concern for maintaining the boundaries that kept outsiders outside and the "lost" lost resulted in their withholding grace from Gentiles, persons whom God created, despite biblical promises that nations (i.e., "Gentiles") would be the recipients of God's salvation (e.g., Isa. 49:6; 60:2-3). Different readers of Acts will relate to each of the characters associated with this story. But the basic question of the story still remains: When God extends God's grace to persons and groups who are often beyond the limits or imaginations of those who are already seen as active participants (at one level or another) within the broader Christian church, how will God's people respond to what God has done and to whom God's grace has found?

Questions for Consideration

1. What do you think are the reasons behind the narrator making sure that we as readers know about Cornelius? Why do you think the narrator gives us more information about Cornelius than about Peter?

2. What might be some reasons for including double visions—one for Cornelius and one for Peter? What do you see as similarities between them? How are they different? What do these things suggest about the role of these visions in the story of Cornelius and Peter?

3. What do you think is behind the criticism of Peter by the Jerusalem believers in Acts 11? How might their concerns relate to the reaction of those who accompanied Peter to Cornelius's house when the Spirit came upon the Gentiles?

---

17. I contend that Luke connects these Jewish believers together. See Thompson, *Keeping the Church*, 142-43, and Thompson, *Acts*, 214-15.

4. What things do you see repeated in the three accounts of the story of Cornelius and Peter (Acts 10, 11, and 15)? What things do you see that drop out? What do these suggest?

5. Today's church does not deal with questions about Jews and Gentiles. However, the church still faces questions about who might be considered part of the church and who might not. How might the church respond in ways that remains open to God's guidance and grace among all people?

E. Differences between Acts and the Pauline Letters: Introduction

We all know that readers approach the Bible with presuppositions. And we as readers even come to the Bible with many stories already formed in our minds. For instance, if someone asked you to describe what happened on the first Easter Sunday, there is little doubt that we all could recite many of the things that we affirm as Christians: the empty tomb, the stone that had been rolled away, the declaration that Jesus has been raised, and other things. And yet when we examine the various accounts found in the four New Testament Gospels, there are differences (both small and large) that we cannot and should not ignore or sweep under the rug. To be sure, these differences are not what matters most when reading these Gospels and these accounts about Jesus's resurrection. Yet, at the same time, we still have *different* accounts in *different* Gospels that contribute together to provide us *different* portraits of Jesus.[1] And the only way that we have access to these different portraits is by *reading* these different accounts, whereby we respect the differences found in each Gospel by allowing them to stand within the respective Gospel (narrative) text and to contribute to that developing picture before us.

---

1. See Luke Timothy Johnson, *Living Jesus: Learning the Heart of the Gospel* (San Francisco: HarperSanFrancisco, 1999), 119-28, where he describes how the Gospel writers are much like painters who are not confined to reproducing photographs but who utilize available artistic (or literary) techniques to capture the essences or souls of their subjects.

When we try to eliminate the differences or when we interpret one Gospel through a larger, homogenized Gospel that combines indiscriminately the different scenes and emphases of our four New Testament Gospels, we end up settling for something other than what each of the four Gospels may potentially say to us. In many ways, we end up creating our personal versions of the *Diatessaron*,[2] which Tatian (in the second century) created from these four Gospels and which the church rejected in favor of the acceptance and embrace of four different Gospels *together*. Yet in doing what Tatian did, we run the risk of missing what is truly good news from Luke's perspective or even from Matthew's. For instance, look what happens during the Advent season? Our manger scenes combine elements from Luke's account of Jesus's birth and other elements from the Matthean Gospel. In the process, although we see something significant about the incarnation, we can easily miss what each Gospel contributes uniquely yet differently that is truly good news.

> **Just like we run the risk of misreading or misinterpreting one particular Gospel when we interpret it through the lens of a different Gospel, we also run the risk of misreading Acts when we interpret it through the lens of the Pauline corpus.**

So what does this have to do with the book of Acts? Think about Paul and his ministry, and consider some basic questions about him: How would you describe Paul? What do you know about him as a person? What do you know about his background? What role did Paul play in the early days of the Christian movement? To whom did he minister? The main sources for the answers to these questions include, not surprisingly, the book of Acts *and* the letters within the Pauline corpus of the New Testament. What typically happens is that as we answer questions like the ones mentioned above, we combine the information we have gleaned from these different materials. And yet, as has been recognized

---

2. The *Diatessaron* combined the four Gospels into a single narrative (a harmony of the Gospels).

for decades now, differences exist between the book of Acts and the Pauline Letters that we cannot easily combine together or explain away. There is little doubt that one can account for most of these differences in the respective perspectives and purposes of the different authors and materials.[3] But just like we run the risk of misreading or misinterpreting one particular Gospel when we interpret it through the lens of a different Gospel, we also run the risk of misreading Acts when we interpret it through the lens of the Pauline corpus.[4]

A good example of the problems of interpreting Acts according to the perspective of Paul's letter can be found in interpretations of the nature of "tongues" in Acts 2 and 1 Corinthians 14. Interpreters of Acts 2 often ignore the fact that the term translated "native language" (*dialektos*) seems to be used as a synonym for another word in the passage that is translated "tongue" (*glōssa*). Instead of associating these two synonymous words in the same chapter, they opt to connect the latter word with Paul's use of that same term in 1 Corinthians 14. Such interpretations easily misread the Acts passage by failing to recognize that different authors may use the same word differently. And one sees similar kinds of flawed readings in the other direction, with interpreters reading Paul's mention of tongues speaking as a reference to human languages, based on Luke's depiction of Pentecost in Acts 2. In both instances, there is a failure to take seriously the literary context of each respective text, and in the process, interpreters make erroneous connections between two texts that are likely referring to very different things.

None of this means that we should never read Acts in light of Paul's letters (or the other way around). However, this *does* mean that in reading and studying the Pauline portion of Acts, interpreters must use critical care and discernment

---

3. Because of the dominance of historical criticism within biblical studies in recent centuries, biblical scholars have tended to give historical preference to Paul over Acts. As a result, Acts has often been viewed in a less-than-favorable light when it differs from Paul's letters. However, such conclusions are now viewed as inadequate because both authors presented images of Paul consistent with their respective perspectives and rhetorical purposes.

4. Of course, the opposite is also true: that we run the risk of misinterpreting a Pauline letter by reading it through the lens of the Acts narrative.

to recognize the *Lukan* characterization of Paul rather than see some form of the *Pauline* self-characterization in Acts. This likewise means acknowledging a *Lukan* depiction and perspective of events and situations instead of reading a *Pauline* point of view into Acts. Similarities will naturally abound, too, but both these similarities and differences must be considered within the context of the tendencies and purposes of Acts.[5] If we are truly seeking to read and interpret *Acts*, then we must take seriously what *that* narrative has to say about Paul and more importantly about God and God's purposes for an expanding understanding of God's people.

---

5. For a thorough assessment of similarities and differences between Acts and the Pauline Letters, see Thomas E. Phillips, *Paul, His Letters, and Acts*, Library of Pauline Studies (Peabody, MA: Hendrickson, 2009).

10

The Acts 15 Account of the Jerusalem Council in Comparison to Galatians 1–2

The differences between the book of Acts and the Pauline Letters must be adequately addressed so that the reader may study and interpret the specific text in ways that give primacy to that text's details. If a person is interpreting the book of Acts, he or she may refer to the Pauline Letters in that interpretive task only *(a)* if those letters are used to supplement the Acts materials, *(b)* if the use of those letters does not replace or revise textual details and information found in Acts, and *(c)* if the use of those letters fills in gaps in Acts in ways that are consistent with other portions of Acts.

One of the most significant areas of scholarly interest about the relationship between Acts and the Pauline corpus has to do with the so-called Jerusalem Council, which we find described in Acts 15. The significance of this meeting of the Jerusalem church within the Acts narrative cannot be minimized, given the nature of the controversy, its placement at the heart of the narrative, and the additional reference to the council's decision later in Acts 21. However, like the absence of any mention of the Pentecost event elsewhere in the New Testament, the relative silence about that meeting in the letters of Paul, given the importance of it for Paul's ministry in Acts, creates some unavoidable questions.

That being stated, Galatians 2:1-10 is one passage that many (but certainly not all) biblical scholars understand as the only likely Pauline reference to the meeting of the Jerusalem Council. When one carefully compares that passage in Galatians 2 with Acts 15, one can begin to see why scholars have found reasons for associating them together (although some interpreters have concluded that the Galatians passage refers to an earlier meeting that the Acts narrative scarcely mentions [see Acts 11:30]).[1]

However, if readers assume that these two passages are different renditions of the same meeting in Jerusalem, then the larger question presents itself: How best should readers proceed with the interpretive task? Like what often occurs when reading and interpreting the Gospels (and Acts), readers try to find out what really happened. Interpreters often proceed in the interpretive task with the assumption that if they find out what *really* happened, then that will clear up everything else: misunderstandings, theological confusion, questions about how to live, and so on. But this approach begins with a basic problem: asking *historical* questions that deal with events and situations behind the text. Historical questions are important, but those issues may not help us deal with the pressing question about *the specific literary text in front of us* and its purposes.[2]

In the end, interpretive questions should focus on the text of Acts itself, which means that we must deal with the distinctive Lukan perspective and rendition of that event as it appears in Acts 15. To state this does not diminish the comparative work between the Galatians and Acts versions. Just like the comparison between two Gospel versions of the same event, our work in assessing the two versions of the meeting in Jerusalem can help us to *(a)* discover (potentially) different understandings of the same event, *(b)* recognize the distinctive emphases and omissions in the version of Acts 15, and *(c)* clarify important themes and messages that arise from Acts 15. But such work stands

---

1. See ibid., 50-82, for a detailed assessment of Paul's chronology in Acts and Paul's letters.

2. Such historical-critical work that attempts to "synchronize" the Acts 15 and Galatians 2 passages is readily available in many commentaries. However, that is not the focus of this reading.

in stark contrast to readings of Acts that are filtered through the perspective of the Pauline Letters.

Paul's Rendition of the Jerusalem Council (Gal. 2:1-10)

Let's begin with Paul's version of the Jerusalem Council in Galatians 2. Paul's account continues an autobiographical portion of the letter that outlines the transformation of his life from persecutor of the church (1:13-14) to proclaimer of the gospel to the Gentiles (vv. 15-16, 23). His emphasis on not seeing apostles during one visit to Jerusalem (except for a fifteen-day visit with Peter—whom he identifies as Cephas—and briefly seeing James) confirms his assertion that he was not acquainted with the churches or church leaders around Jerusalem (vv. 19-23). The likely reason for Paul's "invisibility" to those within Jewish church circles was that his ministry focused on the north: in Syria and Cilicia (v. 21).

Paul's letter recounts a trip to Jerusalem after fourteen years[3] that was prompted by a "revelation," which emphasizes divine initiative (not human decision) as the ultimate reason behind it (2:2). He mentions nothing about the substance of that revelation or why he took Barnabas and Titus with him (vv. 1-2). However, Paul briefly describes what happened in Jerusalem: he met privately with church leaders, explaining the gospel that he had proclaimed among the Gentiles (v. 2).[4] Although Paul need not further expound for his Galatian audience what that message was, his disclosure that they did not force the requirement of circumcision upon the Gentile believer Titus offers readers some clues about what he told them (v. 3).[5]

---

3. The time span may indicate how long it had been since Paul's conversion or call (Gal. 2:1; see 1:15-16). See George Lyons, *Galatians: A Commentary in the Wesleyan Tradition*, New Beacon Bible Commentary (Kansas City: Beacon Hill Press of Kansas City, 2012), 100-101.

4. See J. Louis Martyn, *Galatians: A New Translation with Introduction and Commentary*, The Anchor Bible 33A (New York: Doubleday, 1997), 188-99, who sees this meeting as separate from an initial public meeting (much like what is described in Acts 15).

5. Paul understood these actions as a confirmation of his gospel message: a Gentile was not required to become Jewish to be Christian. See Hans Dieter Betz, *Galatians: A Commentary on Paul's Letter to the Churches in Galatia*, Hermeneia (Philadelphia: Fortress, 1979), 88.

The mention of a group whom Paul characterizes as "false brothers" (*pseudadelphous*) who had "slipped in secretly" for purposes of "spying on our freedom" (v. 4, AT) suggests that some persons had very different ideas about the role of the Jewish law for all believers, including Gentile believers. From Paul's perspective, their tactic appeared to be underhanded and untrustworthy, even though they may have seemed and sounded differently to others.[6] The broader Greek sentence makes it unclear whether the infiltration of these intruders occurred in Jerusalem during Paul's meeting with the church leaders (vv. 2-3) or at some prior point during Paul's ministry in Syria and Cilicia (i.e., in Antioch [1:21-24]).[7] However, the word order implies that these intruders confronted Paul and the church leaders during the meeting with what Paul understood as a challenge to the "truth of the gospel" (2:5), which from his perspective threatened the believers' "freedom . . . in Christ Jesus" (v. 4).

The remainder of Paul's account offers his conclusions about the meeting in Jerusalem (vv. 6-10). First, Paul admitted that the leaders neither added anything to his message nor changed anything about it (v. 6). This confirms his earlier stance: that God, not humans, was the source of his message and mission (1:16-17). This also clarified that God shows no favoritism (2:6) by deferring to some leaders over others like Paul. Second, the church leaders recognized Paul's distinct mission and call as an "apostle to the Gentiles" or "to the uncircumcised" in contrast to Peter's distinct work as an "apostle to the circumcised" (vv. 7-8). Third, the "pillars" or key leaders of the church in Jerusalem—James, Peter, and John—also recognized how God's grace was at

---

6. The adjective translated "brought in secretly" (*pareisaktos* [CEB]) was often used to describe acts of military or political conspiracy. The verb translated "slipped in" (*pareiserchomai* [CEB]) connotes intruders who had their own agenda. See Lyons, *Galatians*, 111: "The 'spies' did not go unnoticed. Only their sinister designs and traitorous allegiances were unsuspected before this incident."

7. See, e.g., F. F. Bruce, *The Epistle to the Galatians: A Commentary on the Greek Text*, New International Greek Testament Commentary (Grand Rapids: Eerdmans, 1982), 114; Richard N. Longenecker, *Galatians*, Word Biblical Commentary 41 (Dallas: Word, 1990), 50-52; Lyons, *Galatians*, 103-4; and Martyn, *Galatians*, 188. For a classic treatment of this issue, see Kirsopp Lake, "The Apostolic Council in Jerusalem," in *Additional Notes to the Commentary on Acts*, ed. K. Lake and H. J. Cadbury, vol. 5 of *The Acts of the Apostles*, ed. F. J. Foakes-Jackson and K. Lake, The Beginnings of Christianity 1 (London: Macmillan, 1933), 195-99.

work in the ministry of Paul and Barnabas (v. 9). By extending the right hand of fellowship, these leaders considered Paul and Barnabas as equal partners in ministry as they all served different constituencies: Paul and Barnabas would continue to minister to Gentiles (i.e., the uncircumcised, including those who were not expected to become Jewish before or after coming to faith in Christ); and the other leaders, to the Jewish people (v. 9). Fourth, the reminder about caring for the poor (presumably in Jerusalem) emphasized not only the importance of hospitality and charitable giving but also the church's solidarity, since all believers (both Jewish and Gentile) responded in the fulfillment of prophetic expectations that the salvation of Israel and the nations (or Gentiles) would include the blessing of God's people in Jerusalem (see, e.g., Isa. 45:14; 60:5-17; 61:6; Hag. 2:6-9).[8]

Luke's Version of the Jerusalem Council (Acts 15)

Because Luke's rendition of the Jerusalem Council is much more extensive than the brief account that Paul offers in Galatians, it stands to reason that the Acts version includes much more detail about the meeting. Thus for our purposes attention will be given to major differences and emphases in the Lukan account.

First, the Lukan narrator emphasizes a different reason for the meeting. Paul in Galatians refers to God's prompting through a "revelation" (Gal. 2:2) that led to his trip to Jerusalem. But Luke refers to unnamed persons from Judea who took it upon themselves to go to Antioch—the first site of extensive ministry efforts including both Jewish and Gentile believers in Acts (see Acts 11:19-30) *and* the church that sent Paul and Barnabas on their first preaching mission into the empire (13:1-3; 14:26-28)—and remediate their work. The message of these "self-ordained" teachers contradicted the essence and results of the ministry of Paul and Barnabas, stating that the Gentile believers must

---

8. See Lyons, *Galatians*, 122.

become Jewish or they could not possibly be saved (see 15:1-2). This controversy (which echoes Paul's report about the "false brothers" in Gal. 2:4-5 [AT]) led to the Antioch church sending Paul and others to Jerusalem to consult about the matter (Acts 15:2-3).

Second, Luke's version describes *two* meetings (rather than one) in Jerusalem: one was larger and more "public" in nature (vv. 4-5), and the second was more private and limited to church leaders along with Paul and Barnabas (vv. 6-21). Luke only mentions three things about the first meeting: the church welcomed Paul and Barnabas, the pair reported what God had done in their ministry (a Lukan allusion to Acts 13 and 14), and then the proceedings were seemingly interrupted by those claiming that the church must require Gentile believers to keep the law of Moses, including circumcision (15:5).[9] The abrupt shift from the larger meeting to a smaller, private meeting suggests what Luke conveniently leaves out: that the interjection of this claim stirred up more than a little controversy and debate among those who were gathered.

Third, Luke's version of the Jerusalem Council centers on the ensuing debate within that smaller meeting. Although it is not surprising that Paul's letter also highlights his insistence on maintaining a position about the gospel that would not require circumcision for Gentile believers (see Gal. 2:3-5), Luke's account reports this emphasis as first coming from *Peter*, who offered a theological interpretation of his experiences at the home of the Gentile Cornelius (Acts 15:7-11; cf. 10:1-48). From the lips of Peter in Acts, both the council and readers of Acts hear that God chose *Peter* as the one "through whom the Gentiles would hear the message of the good news and become believers" (15:7, NRSVue). To be sure, the ministry pair of Barnabas and Paul followed

---

9. Unlike Paul, who refers to "false believers" who seemingly challenged his ministry and version of the gospel (see Gal. 2:4-5), Luke refers to "some believers who belonged to the sect of the Pharisees" (Acts 15:5, NRSVue). Although Luke's characterization of these "interrupters" may initially appear as less polemical, one should remember that Luke's perspective toward Pharisees is not always positive. In this instance, they oppose all in the last five chapters that Luke has linked to the will and guidance of God. See Thompson, *Keeping the Church*, 185, and John A. Darr, *On Character Building: The Reader and the Rhetoric of Characterization in Luke-Acts*, Literary Currents in Biblical Interpretation (Louisville, KY: Westminster/John Knox, 1992), 120-21.

up with their own report about God, salvation, and the Gentiles, but even Luke only summarizes it (v. 12).[10]

Now let's be clear: Luke's primary concern in this section is about Gentile inclusion, not about which person gets credit for the idea. As Luke continues to describe the meeting, Peter's testimony as an apostle was more influential and authoritative among the leaders (with the testimony of Barnabas and Paul functioning in more of a supportive role).[11] Despite Paul's own claims about apostleship in his letters, Paul at this point in Acts has a different (albeit important) role, one that is still secondary to the apostles.[12]

Fourth, a key element of the council's debate is James's noteworthy comments and recommendation. One reason why his comments are noteworthy is because he confirms God's work among the Gentiles by describing a visitation from God, a common Old Testament image of God's intervention and deliverance on behalf of God's people.[13] But that same divine work was creating and making Gentiles (lit. "the nations") into "a people" (the word Luke uses for God's people) (v. 14). Another reason why his comments are noteworthy is because of his reappropriation and reinterpretation of the Hebrew Scriptures.[14] When James quoted the passage from Amos 9:11-12, he reinterpreted it in

---

10. Although the Lukan narrator describes the report by Barnabas and Paul in terms of what God had done "among the Gentiles" (Acts 15:12), it is doubtful that this expression meant that no Jewish persons were included or part of their ministry. Throughout their ministry in chapters 13 and 14, they ministered to both Jewish and Gentile persons. However, the issue before the Jerusalem Council was not about Jewish believers but only about Gentile believers. That is likely the reason for the emphasis on Gentiles by Peter, Barnabas, and Paul in Acts 15.

11. Note that James does not even acknowledge the testimony of Barnabas and Paul but likely acknowledges that of Peter (if the reference to Simeon was about Simon Peter; see Gaventa, *Acts of the Apostles*, 218, and Thompson, *Acts*, 264-65).

12. Readers should note that, in Acts, Paul does not qualify as an apostle (see the criteria for apostleship in 1:21-23). Therefore, the Lukan author refrains from assigning him that title. The two places where the word "apostle" is used to describe him (14:4, 14) also refer to Barnabas, so it is not used in such an "official" way there.

13. See, e.g., Genesis 21:1; 50:24-25; Exodus 3:16; 4:31; 13:19; 32:34; 1 Samuel 2:21; Jeremiah 5:29; 9:8, 24; 11:22.

14. Biblical scholars continue to debate the issue of the specific version of Amos 9 that the Lukan narrator includes in this account of the Jerusalem Council, since the Septuagint's rendering of that passage is offered, rather than the Hebrew version, which "adapts" or changes parts of the Hebrew text. See, e.g., Carl R. Holladay, *Acts: A Commentary*, The New Testament Library (Louisville, KY: Westminster/John Knox, 2016), 301-2; Craig S. Keener, *Acts: An Exegetical Commentary*, 4 vols. (Grand Rapids: Baker Academic, 2012-15), 3:2245-58; and Robert C. Tannehill, *The Narrative Unity of Luke-Acts: A Literary Interpretation*, vol. 2, *The Acts of the Apostles* (Minneapolis: Fortress, 1990), 187-89.

light of what the church seemed to discern as God's work and mission. Readers should note that James did not make the error of twisting or manipulating the biblical text to suit himself. Rather, James offered a fresh reading and interpretation of the passage because of what the collective community of faith understood as the work of God. That is, because of the faith community's collective understanding of God's activity among the Gentiles, James suggested that the church return to the passage and reconsider its message for the church. This is not unlike John Wesley's insistence about the role of experience in testing the interpretation of Scripture, which may direct prayerful readers of Scripture back to *re*read and *re*interpret passages of Scripture that they thought they understood.[15]

James's recommendation for Gentile believers generally corresponds both with the Lukan description of the ministry of Paul and Barnabas and also with Paul's gospel considerations in Galatians 2. The inference behind the introduction to James's recommendation is that the requirement for Gentile believers that some Jewish believers interjected into the meeting in Jerusalem—that Gentile believers must become Jewish and follow the Jewish law—would create problems that those Gentile believers could not overcome (Acts 15:19). However, it was also unlikely that all the believers in Jerusalem endorsed the recommendation, as this contradicted the controversial claim that provoked the debate (cf. v. 5). Nonetheless, James's suggested recommendation for Gentiles has often puzzled later readers of Acts because Luke includes no rationale for those specific "requirements" or guidelines. It is likely that James's instructions for Gentile believers provided them pastoral guidance to avoid key practices that were typically associated with idolatry.[16] Since these four suggestions were part of the so-called Holiness Code (Lev. 17–18) and addressed Gentiles living

---

15. For a brief delineation about the role of experience within John Wesley's theological reflection, see Randy L. Maddox, *Responsible Grace: John Wesley's Practical Theology* (Nashville: Kingswood, 1994), 44-46.

16. The slight differences between the three versions of the list or so-called Apostolic Decree (Acts 15:20; 29; 21:25) suggest that the function of the *whole*, rather than the *specific* guidelines, is most important.

among the Jewish people, God-fearing Gentiles (i.e., those who worshipped at Jewish synagogues) were already familiar with such matters and probably were accustomed to living by them.

Fifth, the Lukan summary about the sending of the letter (with the decree) to the Antioch church along with representatives from the Jerusalem church, Paul, and Barnabas underscores the cooperation among all the believers. Despite actions that could have fractured the believers along Jewish and Gen-

> **Despite actions that could have fractured the believers along Jewish and Gentile lines, Luke offers a picture of solidarity, encouragement, and peace.**

tile lines, Luke offers a picture of solidarity, encouragement, and peace (Acts 15:31-34). And Luke depicts Paul and Barnabas continuing to do in Antioch as they had done in the past: ministering faithfully to both Jewish and Gentile persons alike (v. 35).

Themes and Messages from Luke's Version of the Jerusalem Council in Acts 15

In light of this brief assessment of the two accounts of the Jerusalem Council meeting—the Pauline version in his letter to the Galatians (2:1-10) and the Lukan version in Acts 15 (vv. 1-21)—readers should recognize several themes and messages that arise from the Acts 15 version, with some of these emphases being shared (at least in part) by Paul and others.

First, for both Luke and Paul there is a shared concern about conflicting views or understandings about the church as the people of God. Although chronological questions exist as persons try to figure out how the specific details of Acts and Galatians might fit together, both writings generally agree about the presence of a similar problem: that some Jewish believers insisted non-Jewish believers must become Jewish in identity and practice to become or remain part of the church (see Acts 15:1-5; Gal. 2:3-5). For Paul, both in his first-person reports about his ministry (see Gal. 2:2) and in Luke's third-person account about Paul's report to the Jerusalem Council (Acts 15:12), his concern was the recognition of God's saving work among all persons, including the Gentiles. For most Jewish persons, such recognition was beyond the scope of their experience or expectation, so the mere suggestion of the salvation of Gentiles or non-Jewish persons was an unexpected, "foreign" concept for them. This required nothing less than a "conversion" of sorts that would reorient their outlook, perspective, and imagination about what God and God's grace might do beyond their limited vision. Such difficulties are not unique to the first-century church, since they arise within the contemporary church when persons struggle to recognize God and God's grace at work among others whom God might bless and sanctify for God's purposes.

Second, the Lukan depiction of this understanding about God and the expanding mission of God offers a slightly different perspective from what Paul suggests in Galatians. Both Galatians and Acts share a perspective that affirms the expanding church as inclusive of all people, including both Jewish and Gentile believers. But whereas Galatians depicts what may be described as "segregated" ministry, with Peter ministering to Jewish persons and Paul to Gentile persons, the Lukan perspective offers a more integrated, holistic approach to ministry, with Paul ministering to Jewish and Gentile persons alike (which is consistent with the initial version of his call; see Acts 9:15-16). And James's recommendation to the Gentile believers seems to respond pastorally to ensure genuine, nurturing fellowship between them and their Jewish counterparts (15:19-21, 28-29). Thus the Lukan narrator continues to depict Paul's mission and ministry to both Jews and Gentiles, unlike what Paul himself suggests in Galatians.[17] Accordingly, the Lukan perspective in Acts focuses on a broader understanding of Paul's mission and ministry, presenting God as working

---

17. A common error among interpreters of Acts is the description of Paul's mission as a "mission to the Gentiles," which reflects Paul's perspective in his letters (e.g., Galatians) more than Luke's perspective in Acts.

among *all* people and creating the church as the people of God from among them *all.*

Third, Luke's portrayal of the church, the church's apostles, and the authority of those apostles is different from Paul's. On the one hand, Paul in Galatians affirms his own authority as an apostle because of the revelation and calling that he received directly from God (see Gal. 1:1, 11-12, 15-17). And Paul in Galatians implies that he exercised that authority during the Jerusalem Council (see 2:3-5). On the other hand, Luke in Acts describes Paul as a transformed preacher of the gospel and witness to the resurrection of Jesus (see Acts 9:1-22). But when he traveled to Jerusalem, the apostles and elders served as leaders of the church. Although Paul *addressed* those leaders, Luke's depiction of the meeting subtly suggests that Paul was not numbered among them, since both Peter and James occupied more significant roles in that meeting than Paul (15:6-21). Nonetheless, in Acts readers discover a wholesome trust in the church's process and deliberations as it wrestled to discern God's will. This Lukan picture of the church and its leadership in that moment provides readers a glimpse into how the Spirit guides the people of God collectively in the midst of new and complicated circumstances.

Fourth, the Lukan depiction of the place of Scripture within the Jerusalem Council helps both readers of Acts and the contemporary church see how to engage Scripture when facing complex and unique challenges that arise in ministry. The Jerusalem Council was ultimately a meeting that was tasked with doing theology. They had debated and heard reports that God was working among the Gentiles (as they assumed God was working among the Jewish people). One could argue that they were good Wesleyans, since tradition, reason, and experience were already in the mix of their deliberations when James spoke up and mentioned (or told them to remember) the Amos passage! But they considered the experience of Peter (Acts 15:7-11) and also of Barnabas and Paul (v. 12) collectively before James spoke up. And his proposal ensured that tradition played a key role in their discernment process so that their endorsement of something new did not somehow make the old extraneous or irrelevant.[18] Thus their experience did not treat Scripture as secondary in importance, but their experience invited them to return to reread, rethink, and reengage that Scripture in light of what they understood God was doing. Their fresh reading of Amos came out of an emerging sense of God's saving activity among the Gentiles that they shared together.[19] Perhaps the Spirit of God might call the contemporary church to a similar rereading and rethinking of Scripture (especially those passages about whose meanings the church is so confident) when evidence exists that points to God working in new and surprising ways.

Conclusion

It is very easy for other influences to affect how readers of Acts engage the narrative before them. And these influences—whether acknowledged or not—add to what the Lukan narrator offers as the narrative world of Acts. Sometimes the narrator may allude to cultural ideas or images outside of Acts under assumption that readers would know and share these ideas or images. But other times, readers may bring ideas with them that color their reading of Acts. And for Luke's account of the Jerusalem Council in Acts 15 (as well as other portions of the Pauline portion of Acts), interpreters insert ideas from Paul's letters into their reading of Acts—ideas that may be incompatible with the Lukan narrative and may alter their understanding of the text itself. But by giving attention to the narrative of Acts alone, readers of Acts can engage *that* text as part of the church's sacred Scriptures.

---

18. See Robert W. Wall, "The Acts of the Apostles: Introduction, Commentary, and Reflections," in *The New Interpreter's Bible*, 12 vols., ed. L. Keck (Nashville: Abingdon, 2002), 10:211-12.

19. See Thompson, *Acts*, 270-71.

Questions for Consideration

1. What do you think was the central issue that caused the Jerusalem Council to convene?

2. In what ways do you understand Paul's and Luke's accounts of the Jerusalem Council (in Gal. 2 and Acts 15, respectively) to be similar? Different? And how do these things matter for reading Acts?

3. What do you consider to be the most significant differences when comparing the Lukan version of the Jerusalem Council (Acts 15) to the Pauline version (Gal. 2)? Explain.

4. What would you identify as the two most significant features or emphases of Luke's version of the Jerusalem Council (Acts 15)? Explain.

5. How would you explain the role and appropriation of Scripture in James's comments to the assembly (Acts 15:13-21)? In what way does that Scripture relate to the testimonies of Peter (vv. 7-11) and of Barnabas and Paul (v. 12)?

6. What might be some lessons for the contemporary church from this meeting? From the meeting's interpretation of how and among whom God was at work? From the meeting's use and rereading of Scripture?

11

"Say It Ain't So!": Paul and the Accusations against Him

(ACTS 21)[1]

Several episodes in Acts function strategically in its developing plot. One of these episodes involves the accusations against Stephen, followed by his murder (Acts 6–7). The second involves the rumors and accusations against Paul, followed by his brush with death (Acts 21). The first episode turns the narrative action from Jerusalem to the surrounding regions and ultimately to other parts of the Mediterranean world. The second episode shifts the action from a focus on the church's ministry to Paul's trials and defense. Arguably, these two episodes of accusations against two believers turn the narrative action more abruptly and dramatically, since they reflect and provoke emotion and tension over issues about the nature of the people of God.

What is particularly intriguing about the second episode is the narrative ambiguity that arises when the reader encounters it. To be sure, the Lukan narrator has offered much to the reader with regard to the main character, Paul. But the narrative leaves out more potentially useful information than it includes, which leaves to the reader the task of sorting out the implications and filling in the many gaps. At the heart of these problems are the accusations against Paul:

---

1. For a longer, original version of this chapter, see Richard P. Thompson, "'Say It Ain't So, Paul!': The Accusations against Paul in Acts 21 in the Light of His Ministry in Acts 16–20," *Biblical Research* 45 (2000): 34-50.

that he had taught against Jewish customs, including circumcision, and that he had spoken against the temple. Based on what readers know about Paul, several questions arise. What might be the bases for such accusations? Are these fabricated as were the false accusations against Stephen (6:13), or are they merited? Do the Jerusalem believers think the accusations are accurate? And what does the narrative itself offer that may assist in understanding both this scene and its function in Acts? Unfortunately, the narrative text is largely silent about such matters. The reader may wish to scream about the accusations, "Say it ain't so!"[2] But neither the narrator nor Paul say anything to refute the charges, which further complicates the interpretation of this passage.

Since both the Lukan narrator and Paul are silent about the accusations against Paul, three considerations seem appropriate in an attempt to understand this scene and to listen to its message as Christian Scripture. First, we should begin by examining the accusations themselves within Acts and, more specifically, in comparison with the Lukan characterization of Paul. Second, we should also explore possible connections between this passage in Acts 21 and other episodes that are part of the Acts narrative focusing on Paul's ministry (especially Acts 16–20).[3] Third, after making these connections, we can consider possible ways that this passage can continue to speak to contemporary believers and churches.

Accusations within the Acts Narrative and Acts 21

Paul functions as a reliable character with whom readers of Acts may identify and through whom the Lukan narrator often speaks. Two elements of the characterization of Paul stand out. First, after the encounter with the risen Jesus in Acts 9, Luke presents Paul as someone who was divinely commissioned

---

2. This exclamation was made famous during the so-called Black Sox Scandal, when accusations surfaced that "Shoeless Joe" Jackson and other members of the 1919 Chicago White Sox baseball team conspired to lose the 1919 World Series intentionally.

3. The reason for selecting Acts 16–20, rather than the broader Pauline portion of Acts 13–20, is because the nature of Paul's ministry changes after the Jerusalem Council (Acts 15).

(cf. vv. 15-16) and obedient. That divine commission propelled Paul (with his ministry partners) to proclaim the gospel message throughout the ancient Mediterranean world. Second, the narrative presents Paul as a devout and loyal Jew. His actions and works *in Acts* reflect his fidelity to Judaism and to God. Upon entering a city, his custom was to go to the Jewish synagogue on the Sabbath (see 13:5, 14; 14:1; 16:13; 17:1, 10, 17; 18:4, 19; 19:8). He himself even circumcised Timothy "because of the Jews who lived in those areas" (16:3, CEB). Later in Philippi, the accusations against Paul and his partners provided "outside" confirmation of

> **Some of the Jewish people responded favorably whenever Paul proclaimed the gospel message, while others responded in opposing and even violent ways.**

Luke's portrait of Paul as a loyal Jew (see vv. 19-24). Certainly, the Lukan Paul appears differently in Acts than the Paul presented in the Pauline Letters. But this difference makes the Lukan depiction of Paul as a loyal and devout Jew all the more significant when examining the rumors and accusations against him in Acts.

Conversely, Luke consistently presents the Jewish people in the "Pauline" portion of Acts (i.e., chs. 13–28) as Paul's *opponents*. That portrait is mixed; some of the Jewish people responded favorably whenever Paul proclaimed the gospel message, while others responded in opposing and even violent ways. Instances of violent Jewish opposition typically occurred after the success of that message among a number of both Jews and Gentiles or after Paul indicated his intention to direct his efforts to Gentiles.[4] Readers are left with a picture of the Jewish people divided in their response to the Christian message and who, more generally, stand antithetically against Paul within the narrative. These different portraits of Jewish individuals and people function in Acts to contrast

---

4. The violent opposition to Paul was not in response to the proclamation of Jesus as the Jewish Messiah but in response to the inclusion of Gentiles in the realm of salvation. However, instances of opposition were not exclusive to the Jewish people, since some scenes present non-Jewish persons who opposed Paul.

two images of what it means to be the people of God.[5]

These contrasting portraits of Jews and their potential function in Acts become important as we turn to the episode in Acts 21 because the *Jewish believers in Jerusalem* appear as a prominent character group. Only in Acts 15 and 21 does this group make appearances in the Pauline portion of Acts. An initial question is this: How do the various images of Jews in earlier chapters of Acts (including those found in the summaries in Acts 1–5) affect one's reading of this specific scene? The Lukan narrator begins the account in Acts 21 with a cordial meeting with James and the elders, in which "Paul greeted them and reported . . . what God had done among the Gentiles through his ministry" (v. 19; see vv. 18-19; cf. 15:12).[6] Although the initial narrated response is positive—since those listening to Paul began to praise God in the same way as believers in earlier scenes did (cf. 2:47; 4:21; 11:18; 13:48)—Luke immediately links this to the raising of concerns about Paul's ministries (21:20-21).[7] This juxtaposition of praise and concern quickly turns what appeared as a hospitable meeting into a confrontation that would leave readers of Acts confounded about what just happened.

This is where the first of the accusations against Paul appear: in the context of that meeting with the church leaders in Jerusalem in Acts 21. The accusations themselves are prefaced by a reminder about the "many thousands" of Jewish believers who were also "zealous for the law" (v. 20). Those remarks contrast with the accusations or rumors about Paul: that he was teaching all Jews living among the Gentiles to apostatize from Moses by instructing them neither to

---

5. See Thompson, *Keeping the Church*, 111-15, 157-60, 236-40, 241-48, and Thompson, *Acts*, esp. 171-72, 255-56.

6. Although most translations and interpreters include Acts 21:17 with the paragraph describing the meeting between Paul and the Jerusalem church leaders, this verse likely belongs with the previous paragraph that describes the arrival *and welcome* of Paul and his partners at the home of Mnason (see vv. 15-16). See Thompson, *Acts*, 350-51; also F. F. Bruce, *The Book of the Acts*, rev. ed., The New International Commentary on the New Testament (Grand Rapids: Eerdmans, 1988), 404; and I. Howard Marshall, *The Acts of the Apostles*, Tyndale New Testament Commentaries (Grand Rapids: Eerdmans, 1980), 341-42.

7. This resembles early moments of the Jerusalem Council, when reports about what God had done were followed immediately by demands that Gentiles be circumcised and follow the law of Moses (Acts 15:4-5).

circumcise their children nor to live according to Jewish customs (v. 21).[8] The Greek present tense of the verb translated "teaching" (NASB) suggests that this allegation against Paul was his *regular* practice, not a rare occurrence, thereby accusing him of teaching against the very law about which the Jewish believers were described as zealous. Not only this, the rumor was that Paul's activities extended to "all the Jews who live among the Gentiles" (v. 21). Although an obvious exaggeration about Paul's ministry among Diaspora Jews (since Acts does not recount Paul's ministry so extensively), this heightened concerns about Paul and suggests that the Jerusalem church leaders *themselves* believed those reports to be true.[9]

Despite such allegations, nothing in this account offers a place for Paul to speak into the situation. The leaders repeated what others were saying about Paul and even asked the question, "What about this?" (v. 22, CEB), but no opportunity existed for Paul to jump in and defend himself. As a result, Paul remained silent, with no opportunity to speak. Even the Lukan narrator, who often jumps onto the narrative stage and speaks directly to readers, offers nothing. Rather, the account of the meeting ends with Paul receiving instructions about him participating in (and funding) a rite of purification with four other men, which essentially placed full responsibility on Paul to prove that the accusations were unfounded (vv. 22-24).[10]

The second set of accusations appears near the end of Paul's rite of purification. The narrator describes a hostile encounter at the temple. Paul's accusers were not Jewish believers but Diaspora Jews from the province of Asia who

---

8. Note that the charge was "apostasy from Moses" (*apostasian apo Mōyseōs*), a most serious charge against any Jewish individual. See Charles H. Talbert, *Reading Acts: A Literary and Theological Commentary on the Acts of the Apostles* (New York: Crossroads, 1997), 192.

9. The similarity of the accusations by the church leaders (Acts 21:21) and the Jews from Asia (vv. 27-28) implies that all Jews believed the charges and were opponents of Paul. Cf. Robert L. Brawley, *Centering on God: Method and Message in Luke-Acts*, Literary Currents in Biblical Interpretation (Louisville, KY: Westminster/John Knox, 1990), 99; Jacob Jervell, *Luke and the People of God: A New Look at Luke-Acts* (Minneapolis: Augsburg, 1972), 194; and Joseph B. Tyson, *Images of Judaism in Luke-Acts* (Columbia, SC: University of South Carolina Press, 1992), 161-62.

10. See Tannehill, *Narrative Unity of Luke-Acts*, 2:270-71, who states that "Paul is risking his life in order to make clear that he affirms the rights of Jewish Christians to live according to the law."

stirred up others at the temple with their charges. Their accusations (v. 28) appear similar to the earlier reports in three ways. First, they found fault with Paul's teaching (cf. v. 21). Second, their concern was that Paul taught "against the law" (cf. v. 21). Third, the audience of Paul's alleged teaching was described in exaggerated ways as "everyone everywhere," including both Jews and even non-Jews (v. 28; cf. 21:20). This claim expanded the charges to allege that Paul taught all persons—both Jews and Gentiles alike—against the Jewish law and customs, the ultimate sign of disloyalty and apostasy against his own people.[11] In support of this claim, they accused him of bringing Greeks (or non-Jews) into the temple (v. 28). These allegations convinced bystanders, resulting in a violent, chaotic scene. The entire city was so aroused that people stormed the temple, seized Paul, and dragged him out of the temple to kill him (v. 30). Only the intervention by Roman soldiers prevented Paul's murder at the hands of this raging mob (vv. 31-33).

The similarities between these two accusations against Paul suggest that both the Jewish believers and the other Jews in Jerusalem viewed him with suspicion over the same basic issues. These similarities have led to a general conclusion by recent scholars that readers of Acts would link together these responses of the believing and nonbelieving Jews here in the narrative.[12] The nonbelieving Jews of the Diaspora were accusing Paul directly, but the believing Jews assumed the validity of such accusations, did nothing to discredit them, and did not give Paul opportunity to speak against the charges. Given the similarities between the accusations and the surprising silence of any protection of Paul or assistance to him from the Christian Jews within the ensuing mob scene at the temple, the distinctions between the two groups of Jews seem to be blurred in the narrative. Therefore, when the narrative described "the whole crowd" as stirred up (v. 27), "the whole city" as aroused (v. 30), and "all Jerusalem" in confusion (v.

---

11. Cf. Brawley, *Centering on God*, 104.
12. See, e.g., Tyson, *Images of Judaism*, 162.

31, NRSVue), is the reader to understand these descriptions as including *both* the non-Christian Jews *and* the Christian Jews? Does the Lukan description of the whole populace of Jerusalem reacting violently against Paul also include the Jewish believers? Where were the Jewish believers when Paul was attacked while doing what they asked of him?[13] Luke mentions nothing.[14] And this leaves the reader to fill in the gaps where silence remains.

Connections between the Accusations of Acts 21 and Acts 16–20

Most interpreters of Acts have supported one of three conclusions about these accusations. Many interpreters contend that these accusations were invalid or unbelievable when compared to Luke's characterization of Paul as a devout, loyal Jew in Acts.[15] Others suggest that the accusations depict the Jewish believers in Jerusalem and the nonbelieving Jews similarly.[16] Still others see the accusations as consistent with what Paul himself wrote and likely taught about circumcision.[17] The first two types of interpretations focus on the unbelievability of the accusations against Paul, *based on Luke's narrative work in Acts*. The last type focuses on the believability of the accusations, *based on the Pauline writings*. What is most problematic about the last type of interpretation is that readers may easily, even unknowingly, replace the Lukan narrative and what it offers by importing information and perspectives that are not part of

---

13. See Johnson, *Acts of the Apostles*, 379: "But by posing this 'challenge from within,' Luke can account for the odd request from the leadership (it is under pressure for its zealous majority) and for Paul's presence in the Temple, as well as why once he is arrested, Paul is not helped by the community as such: it was divided from within concerning Paul's loyalty to Judaism."

14. Contra Richard Bauckham, "James and the Jerusalem Church," in *The Book of Acts in Its Palestinian Setting*, ed. R. Bauckham, The Book of Acts in Its First Century Setting 4 (Grand Rapids: Eerdmans, 1995), 478-79, who states that Luke did not record everything that happened and so the actions of the Christian leaders were not important here.

15. See, e.g., Johnson, *Acts of the Apostles*, 375; B. J. Oropeza, *In the Footsteps of Judas and Other Defectors: The Gospels, Acts, and Johannine Letters*, Apostasy in the New Testament Communities 1 (Eugene, OR: Cascade, 2011), 124; and Wall, "Acts of the Apostles," 10:293.

16. See, e.g., Jack T. Sanders, *The Jews in Luke-Acts* (Philadelphia: Fortress, 1987), 284, and Tyson, *Images of Judaism*, 162.

17. See, e.g., Bruce, *Book of the Acts*, 405, and Richard I. Pervo, *Acts: A Commentary*, Hermeneia (Minneapolis: Fortress, 2009), 544.

the broader narrative world of Acts. But none of these options considers wheth-er evidence exists *within Acts itself* in support of the allegations against Paul. That is, one should ask, Based on the Acts narrative (and not Paul's letters), is there something in the Lukan presentation of Paul's ministry, seen from anoth-er perspective, that could have been understood in the way reflected by those accusations against him?

One way to respond to this question is to look for clues in Acts 21. Two details stand out: the narrator identifies Paul's accusers as "Jews from the prov-ince of Asia" (v. 27, CEB), and this also explains why they assumed Paul defiled the temple (v. 29). Central to that assumption was their earlier sighting of Paul with the Ephesian Trophimus. These details add little to the scene, but the information about Asia and Ephesus invites readers to recall what happened when Paul ministered there. More specifically, the Lukan summary about Paul's Ephesian ministry (19:8-10) underscores what Paul typically did upon enter-ing a city: (1) he went to the synagogue, (2) he proclaimed the gospel, (3) some Jews and Gentiles responded positively, and then (4) some sort of Jewish rejection or opposition arose later. However, one significant difference appears in that summary that may also explain why Paul's ministry in Ephesus lasted much longer than in other cities. In Ephesus, Paul did not leave town after Jewish rejection or opposition but instead left the synagogue as the context for his ministry (see v. 9).

However, Paul's departure from the synagogue may have been more signif-icant than what first meets the contemporary reader's eye. On the one hand, readers of Acts would recognize that Paul's move from the synagogue was not his idea at all but was precipitated by the hostilities of the Jewish opposition. On the other hand, the Jewish synagogue functioned as a center of Jewish identity and law observance for Diaspora Jews, so a person's departure could easily be interpreted as apostasy and a rejection of Jewish heritage, identity, and community. When one considers that the term "apostasy" is derived from the same participle describing Paul's departing actions (*apostas*), the departure itself seems depicted as anything but amicable for Paul, whom Luke has consistently characterized as a loyal, devout Jew. Thus readers are left with conflicting information: a justified departure, but also wording that suggests something more serious. Might this suggest different perspectives or interpretations of Paul's actions?

Since this scene in Ephesus is the second and last one where Luke describes Paul leaving the synagogue of a city and continuing his ministry outside that context, a brief look at the first scene may offer additional clues in sorting out these perspectives of Paul's practices. That first scene, which took place in Corinth, also follows the basic Lukan pattern of Paul's ministry (see 18:1-17). After the initial opposition and slander against Paul's message (v. 6), Paul lost his composure, "shook out his clothes" as either an act of protest or of breaking off all association with the synagogue, and then left the synagogue by going next door and ministering there (v. 6; see v. 7).[18] Like what later happened in Ephesus, Paul remained in town while ministering in a context outside the synagogue. The Lukan narrator is clear that Jewish opposition prompted Paul's departure, not Paul's own initiative. However, the narrative also includes here, for the first time, allegations or charges against Paul. Although Luke depicts Paul as "teaching . . . the word of God" among the Corinthians (v. 11), his opponents also accused him of persuading or, as the wording (*anapeithō*) may connote, misleading or seducing people to worship God in ways "contrary to the law" (v. 13).

As in Ephesus, the Acts narrative itself reveals differences in perspective about Paul's ministry. The charge here is not identical to those raised by the Asian Jews at the temple, who alleged that Paul was teaching "against the law" (21:28, AT). The phrase translated "contrary to the law" (*para ton nomon*

---

18. The verb *synomoreō* (Acts 18:7) implies both that Paul moved next door and that the building shared a common wall or boundary with the synagogue. See Bruce, *Book of the Acts*, 350, and Thompson, *Acts*, 304.

[18:13]) may imply opposition and relates to the hostility of the phrase "against the law" (*kata . . . tou nomou*) noted in the later accusation (21:28). However, the first phrase also connotes something "beside" or "alongside" another, so that the nuance is that Paul taught in ways contrary to the law because he was working *alongside* it.[19] The narrative picture is unavoidable: Paul's new ministry context was next door, or side by side, to the synagogue. Thus the wording of the allegations against Paul in Corinth suggests how some Jews perceived or interpreted Paul's actions: his ministry placed himself *alongside* the synagogue (as the place where the Jewish law was studied and where God was worshipped) and therefore *against* everything that the synagogue represented. Although Luke depicts Paul in a positive manner in this episode, other perspectives seem possible for a first-century Jew, including a perspective that would interpret the teaching of any Jew who had left the synagogue (especially someone who left as emphatically as Paul!) as nothing less than teaching against God and the law.

> **Perhaps the more important issue in Acts is between two understandings of the people of God: one that focuses on the Jewish people and how God may be working among them and another that focuses more inclusively on what God was (and is) doing among all people, both Jews and Gentiles.**

Reflections on Paul's Ministry in Acts—Past and Present

Does the account of the events in Jerusalem involving Paul and others in Acts 21 open the possibility of reading Paul's ministry in Acts in multiple ways? Two points may be considered here. First, the different interpretations of Paul's

---

19. Both the phrase *para ton nomon* (alongside of/contrary to/against the law) and the corresponding phrase *para tou nomou* (beside/from the law) appear frequently in the writings of Flavius Josephus. For the first phrase, see *Jewish Antiquities* 11.228; 17.150-51; also *Against Apion* 2.219; and *Jewish War* 1.11, 209, 378. For the latter phrase, see *Jewish Antiquities* 4.15; 8.361-62; 17.316; also *Against Apion* 1.43; 2.233, 262; and *Jewish War* 1.649.

ministry and the tensions between them may correlate with different images in Acts of what it means to be the "people of God." Although earlier scholarship contended that these tensions arose between Jewish Christianity and Pauline or Gentile Christianity, perhaps the more important issue in Acts is between two understandings of the people of God: one that focuses on the Jewish people and how God may be working among them and another that focuses more inclusively on what God was (and is) doing among all people, both Jews and Gentiles. Second, these two interpretations may correspond to the tensions between the Jews and Gentiles in the original audience of Acts. Since these tensions were not isolated but escalated throughout Acts, one may suggest that the emotion and anxiety that the narrative evokes may have corresponded with real-life emotions and tensions in early Christian communities.

But one should also not ignore the creative and imaginative ways that such texts may continue to speak creatively and imaginatively as Christian Scripture. On the one hand, the openness of the Lukan narrator to allow alternative perspectives to remain within the Acts narrative is significant. Rather than squelching some of these views or diminishing such perspectives within the story, the narrator gives them space, despite the discomfort and unease that they may create in readers who encounter them. Perhaps the inclusion of alternative viewpoints within Acts helps readers not only to discern such perspectives within the narrative but also to navigate many kinds of differences in their own worlds. On the other hand, the silence of both the Lukan narrator and Paul in the face of accusations allows readers to step imaginatively from the narrative to their own world rather than move in a way that is controlled or limited by the parameters of whatever Paul (or others) might have stated. Luke does not offer a narrative to tell readers what to do but to encourage us to imagine new gospel perspectives.

Questions for Consideration

1. According to the church leaders in Jerusalem, what were the major accusations against Paul? How do those accusations compare and contrast with the allegations made by Diaspora Jews against Paul at the temple?

2. What do you think was the role of the believers in Jerusalem when Paul's life was in danger? What do you think was Luke's intention by describing this scene as he did?

3. How do the accusations against Paul compare and contrast with the description of Paul and his ministry in Acts 16–20? Be specific.

4. What may have been the purpose behind the inclusion of different perspectives of Paul's ministry in the book of Acts? What might that say both to Luke's original audience and to the contemporary church?

Bibliography

Achtemeier, Paul J. "An Elusive Unity: Paul, Acts, and the Early Church." *Catholic Biblical Quarterly* 48, no. 1 (1986): 1-26.

———. *The Quest for Unity in the New Testament Church: A Study in Paul and Acts*. Philadelphia: Fortress, 1987.

Alexander, Loveday C. A. *Acts in Its Ancient Literary Context: A Classicist Looks at the Acts of the Apostles*. Library of New Testament Studies 298. New York: T. and T. Clark, 2005.

———. *The Preface to Luke's Gospel: Literary Convention and Social Context in Luke 1.1–4 and Acts 1.1*. Society for New Testament Studies Monograph Series 78. Cambridge, UK: Cambridge University Press, 1993.

Allen, O. Wesley, Jr. *The Death of Herod: The Narrative and Theological Function of Retribution in Luke-Acts*. Society of Biblical Literature Dissertation Series 158. Atlanta: Scholars, 1997.

Andersen, T. David. "The Meaning of *Echontes Charin Pros* in Acts 2.47." *New Testament Studies* 34 (1988): 604-10.

Aune, David E. *The New Testament in Its Literary Environment*. Library of Early Christianity 8. Philadelphia: Westminster, 1987.

Balch, David L. "The Genre of Luke-Acts: Individual Biography, Adventure Novel, or Political History?" *Southwestern Journal of Theology* 33, no. 1 (Fall 1990): 5-19.

Barreto, Eric D. "A Gospel on the Move: Practice, Proclamation, and Place in Luke-Acts." *Interpretation* 72, no. 2 (April 2018): 175-87.

Barrett, C. K. *A Critical and Exegetical Commentary on the Acts of the Apostles 1–14*. International Critical Commentary. Edinburgh: T. and T. Clark, 1994.

———. *A Critical and Exegetical Commentary on the Acts of the Apostles 15–28*. International Critical Commentary. Edinburgh: T. and T. Clark, 1998.

Bartchy, S. Scott. "Community of Goods in Acts: Idealization or Social Reality?" In *The Future of Early Christianity: Essays in Honor of Helmut Koester*, ed. B. A. Pearson, 309-18. Minneapolis: Fortress, 1991.

Barthes, Roland. "L'analyse structurale du récit: A propos d'Actes X–XI." *Recherches de science religieuse* 58 (1970): 17-37.

Bauckham, Richard, ed. *The Book of Acts in Its Palestinian Setting*. The Book of Acts in Its First Century Setting 4. Grand Rapids: Eerdmans, 1995.

———. "James and the Gentiles (Acts 15.13-21)." In *History, Literature, and Society in the Book of Acts*, ed. B. Witherington III, 154-84. Cambridge, UK: Cambridge University Press, 1996.

———. "James and the Jerusalem Church." In *The Book of Acts in Its Palestinian Setting*, ed. R. Bauckham, 415-80. The Book of Acts in Its First Century Setting 4. Grand Rapids: Eerdmans, 1995.

Baur, Ferdinand Christian. *Paul, the Apostle of Jesus Christ, His Life and Work, His Epistles and His Doctrine: A Contribution to a Critical History of Primitive Christianity*. 2 vols. Translated by E. Zeller. Edited by A. Menzies. London: Williams and Norgate, 1876.

Benoit, Pierre. "Remarques sur les 'sommaires' de Actes 2.42 à 5." In *Aux sources de la tradition Chrétienne: Mélanges offerts à M. Maurice Goguel*, 1-10. Bibliothèque théologique. Paris: Delachaux et Niestlé, 1950.

Betz, Hans Dieter. *Galatians: A Commentary on Paul's Letter to the Churches in Galatia*. Hermeneia. Philadelphia: Fortress, 1979.

Binder, Donald D. *Into the Temple Courts: The Place of the Synagogues in the Second Temple Period*. Society of Biblical Literature Dissertation Series 169. Atlanta: Society of Biblical Literature, 1999.

Blomberg, Craig L. "The Law in Luke-Acts." *Journal for the Study of the New Testament* 22 (1984): 53-80.

Blue, Bradley. "Acts and the House Church." In *The Book of Acts in Its Graeco-Roman Setting*, ed. D. W. J. Gill and C. Gempf, 119-22. The Book of Acts in Its First Century Setting 2. Grand Rapids: Eerdmans, 1994.

Bock, Darrell L. *Acts*. Baker Exegetical Commentary on the New Testament. Grand Rapids: Baker Academic, 2007.

———. *A Theology of Luke and Acts: God's Promised Program, Realized for All Nations*. Biblical Theology of the New Testament. Grand Rapids: Zondervan, 2012.

Boismard, M. É. "Le 'concile' de Jérusalem (Act 15, 1-33)." *Ephemerides theologicae lovanienses* 64 (1988): 433-40.

———. *Les Actes des deux Apôtres*. 6 vols. Etudes bibliques. Paris: J. Gabalda, 1990.

Boismard, M. É., and A. Lamouille. *Le texte occidental des Actes des Apôtres: Reconstitution et réhabilitation*. 2 vols. Paris: Éditions Recherche sur les Civilisations, 1984.

Bovon, François. "Tradition et rédaction en Actes 10, 1-11, 18." *Theologische Zeitschrift* 26 (1970): 22-45.

Brawley, Robert L. *Centering on God: Method and Message in Luke-Acts*. Literary Currents in Biblical Interpretation. Louisville, KY: Westminster/John Knox, 1990.

———. "The God of Promises and the Jews in Luke-Acts." In *Literary Studies in Luke-Acts: Essays in Honor of Joseph B. Tyson*, ed. R. P. Thompson and T. E. Phillips, 279-96. Macon, GA: Mercer University Press, 1998.

———. *Luke-Acts and the Jews: Conflict, Apology, and Conciliation*. Society of Biblical Literature Monograph Series 33. Atlanta: Scholars, 1987.

Brodie, Thomas L. "Luke-Acts as an Imitation and Emulation of the Elijah-Elisha Narrative." In *New Views on Luke and Acts*, ed. E. Richard, 78-85. Collegeville, MN: Liturgical, 1990.

Brown, Jeannine K. *The Gospels as Stories: A Narrative Approach to Matthew, Mark, Luke, and John*. Grand Rapids: Baker Academic, 2020.

Bruce, F. F. *The Acts of the Apostles: The Greek Text with Introduction and Commentary*. 2nd ed. Grand Rapids: Eerdmans, 1984.

———. "The Apostolic Decree of Acts 15." In *Studien zum Text und zur Ethik des Neuen Testaments: Festschrift zum 80. Geburtstag von Heinrich Greeven*, ed. W. Schrage, 115-24. Berlin: Walter de Gruyter, 1986.

————. *The Book of the Acts*. Rev. ed. The New International Commentary on the New Testament. Grand Rapids: Eerdmans, 1988.

————. *The Epistle to the Galatians: A Commentary on the Greek Text*. New International Greek Testament Commentary. Grand Rapids: Eerdmans, 1982.

————. "The Significance of the Speeches for Interpreting Acts." *Southwestern Journal of Theology* 33 (Fall 1990): 20-28.

Buckwalter, H. Douglas. "The Divine Saviour." In *Witness to the Gospel: The Theology of Acts*, ed. I. H. Marshall and D. Peterson, 107-24. Grand Rapids: Eerdmans, 1998.

Burridge, Richard A. *What Are the Gospels? A Comparison with Graeco-Roman Biography*. 2nd ed. The Biblical Resource Series. Grand Rapids: Eerdmans, 2004.

Byron, Gay L. *Symbolic Blackness and Ethnic Difference in Early Christian Literature*. New York: Routledge, 2002.

Cadbury, Henry J. *The Making of Luke-Acts*. New York: Macmillan, 1927 (2nd ed., London: S.P.C.K., 1958; repr., Peabody, MA: Hendrickson, 1999).

————. "The Speeches in Acts." In *Additional Notes to the Commentary on Acts*, ed. K. Lake and H. J. Cadbury, 402-27. Vol. 5 of *The Acts of the Apostles*, ed. F. J. Foakes-Jackson and K. Lake. The Beginnings of Christianity 1. London: Macmillan, 1933.

————. *The Style and Literary Method of Luke*. Harvard Theological Studies 6. Cambridge, MA: Harvard University Press, 1920.

Callan, Terrance. "The Background of the Apostolic Decree (Acts 15:20, 29; 21:25)." *Catholic Biblical Quarterly* 55, no. 2 (1993): 284-97.

————. "The Preface of Luke-Acts and Historiography." *New Testament Studies* 31 (1985): 576-81.

Capper, Brian. "The Palestinian Cultural Context of Earliest Christian Community of Goods." In *The Book of Acts in Its Palestinian Setting*, ed. R. Bauckham, 323-56. The Book of Acts in Its First Century Setting 4. Grand Rapids: Eerdmans, 1995.

————. "Reciprocity and the Ethic of Acts." In *Witness to the Gospel: The Theology of Acts*, ed. I. H. Marshall and D. Peterson, 499-518. Grand Rapids: Eerdmans, 1998.

Carroll, John T. "Luke's Portrayal of the Pharisees." *Catholic Biblical Quarterly* 50, no. 4 (1988): 604-21.

Carter, Charles W., and Ralph Earle. *The Acts of the Apostles*. The Evangelical Bible Commentary. Grand Rapids: Zondervan, 1959.

Cassidy, Richard J. *Society and Politics in the Acts of the Apostles*. Maryknoll, NY: Orbis, 1987.

Cassidy, Richard J., and Philip J. Scharper, eds. *Political Issues in Luke-Acts*. Maryknoll, NY: Orbis, 1983.

Chambers, Kathy. "'Knock, Knock—Who's There?': Acts 12:6-17 as a Comedy of Errors." In *A Feminist Companion to the Acts of the Apostles*, ed. A.-J. Levine with M. Blickenstaff, 89-97. Cleveland, OH: Pilgrim, 2004.

Chance, J. Bradley. *Jerusalem, the Temple, and the New Age in Luke-Acts*. Macon, GA: Mercer University Press, 1988.

Chatman, Seymour B. *Story and Discourse: Narrative Structure in Fiction and Film*. Ithaca, NY: Cornell University Press, 1978.

Clark, Andrew C. "The Role of the Apostles." In *Witness to the Gospel: The Theology of Acts*, ed. I. H. Marshall and D. Peterson, 169-90. Grand Rapids: Eerdmans, 1998.

Co, Maria Anicia. "The Major Summaries in Acts: Acts 2,42-47; 4,32-35; 5,12-16 Linguistic and Literary Relationship." *Ephemerides theologicae lovanienses* 68 (1992): 49-85.

Combet-Galland, Corina. "Actes 4/32–5/11." *Etudes théologiques et religieuses* 52 (1977): 548-53.

Conzelmann, Hans. *Acts of the Apostles*. Translated by J. Limburg, A. T. Kraabel, and D. H. Juel. Hermeneia. Philadelphia: Fortress, 1987.

————. *The Theology of St. Luke*. Translated by G. Buswell. Philadelphia: Fortress, 1961.

Cook, Michael J. "The Mission to the Jews in Acts: Unraveling Luke's 'Myth of the "Myriads."'" In *Luke-Acts and the Jewish People: Eight Critical Perspectives*, ed. J. B. Tyson, 102-23. Minneapolis: Augsburg, 1988.

Culy, Martin M., and Mikeal C. Parsons. *Acts: A Handbook on the Greek Text*. Waco, TX: Baylor University Press, 2003.

Dahl, Nils A. "'A People for His Name' (Acts XV.14)." *New Testament Studies* 4 (1957-58): 319-27.

Danker, Frederick W. "Reciprocity in the Ancient World and in Acts 15:23-29." In *Political Issues in Luke-Acts*, ed. R. J. Cassidy and P. J. Scharper, 49-58. Maryknoll, NY: Orbis, 1983.

Darr, John A. *On Character Building: The Reader and the Rhetoric of Characterization in Luke-Acts*. Literary Currents in Biblical Interpretation. Louisville, KY: Westminster/John Knox, 1992.

Dibelius, Martin. *Studies in the Acts of the Apostles*. Translated by M. Ling. London: SCM Press, 1956.

Dicken, Frank E., and Julia A. Snyder, eds. *Characters and Characterization in Luke-Acts*. Library of New Testament Studies 548. New York: T. and T. Clark, 2016.

Dinkler, Michal Beth. "The Politics of Stephen's Storytelling: Narrative Rhetoric and Reflexivity in Acts 7:2-53." *Zeitschrift für die neutestamentliche Wissenschaft und die Kunde der älteren Kirche* 111, no. 1 (2020): 33-64.

Downing, F. Gerald. "Freedom from the Law in Luke-Acts." *Journal for the Study of the New Testament* 26 (1986): 49-52.

Dunn, James D. G. *The Acts of the Apostles*. Narrative Commentaries. Valley Forge, PA: Trinity, 1996.

———. *Beginning from Jerusalem*. Christianity in the Making. Grand Rapids: Eerdmans, 2009.

———. *The Partings of the Ways: Between Christianity and Judaism and Their Significance for the Character of Christianity*. Philadelphia: Trinity, 1991.

Dupont, Jacques. "'Je rebâtirai la cabane de David qui est tombée' (Ac 15,16=Am 9,11)." *Glaube und Eschatologie: Festscrift für Werner Georg Kümmel*, ed. E. Grässer and O. Merk, 19-32. Tübingen, DEU: Mohr, 1985.

————. *Nouvelles études sur les Actes des Apôtres*. Lectio divina 118. Paris: Éditions du Cerf, 1984.

————. *The Salvation of the Gentiles: Essays on the Acts of the Apostles*. Translated by J. R. Keating. New York: Paulist, 1979.

————. *The Sources of the Acts*. Translated by K. Pond. New York: Herder and Herder, 1964.

————. "Un peuple d'entre les nations (Actes 15.14)." *New Testament Studies* 31 (1985): 321-35.

Earle, Ralph. "The Acts of the Apostles." In vol. 7 of *Beacon Bible Commentary*, 247-598. 10 vols. Edited by A. F. Harper et al. Kansas City: Beacon Hill Press of Kansas City, 1965.

Esler, Philip Francis. *Community and Gospel in Luke-Acts: The Social and Political Motivations of Lucan Theology*. Society for New Testament Studies Monograph Series 57. Cambridge, UK: Cambridge University Press, 1987.

Evans, Craig A., and James A. Sanders. *Luke and Scripture: The Function of Sacred Tradition in Luke-Acts*. Minneapolis: Fortress, 1993.

Fiensy, David A. "The Composition of the Jerusalem Church." In *The Book of Acts in Its Palestinian Setting*, ed. R. Bauckham, 213-36. The Book of Acts in Its First Century Setting 4. Grand Rapids: Eerdmans, 1995.

Fitzmyer, Joseph A. *The Acts of the Apostles: A New Translation with Introduction and Commentary*. The Anchor Bible 31. New York: Doubleday, 1998.

————. *Luke the Theologian: Aspects of His Teaching*. New York: Paulist, 1989.

Foakes-Jackson, F. J. *The Acts of the Apostles*. The Moffatt New Testament Commentary. New York: Harper and Brothers, 1931.

————. "Stephen's Speech in Acts." *Journal of Biblical Literature* 49, no. 3 (1930): 283-86.

Foakes-Jackson, F. J., and Kirsopp Lake, eds. *The Beginnings of Christianity, Part 1: The Acts of the Apostles*. 5 vols. London: Macmillan, 1920-33.

Gager, John G. "Jews, Gentiles, and Synagogues in the Book of Acts." In *Christians among Jews and Gentiles: Essays in Honor of Krister Stendahl on His Sixty-Fifth Birthday*, ed. G. W. E. Nickelsburg with G. W. MacRae, 91-99. Philadelphia: Fortress, 1986.

Garrett, Susan R. "Exodus from Bondage: Luke 9:31 and Acts 12:1-24." *Catholic Biblical Quarterly* 52, no. 4 (1990): 656-80.

Garroway, Joshua D. "'Apostolic Irresistibility' and the Interrupted Speeches in Acts." *Catholic Biblical Quarterly* 74, no. 4 (2012): 738-52.

Gasque, W. W. *A History of the Interpretation of the Acts of the Apostles*. Peabody, MA: Hendrickson, 1989.

Gaventa, Beverly Roberts. *The Acts of the Apostles*. Abingdon New Testament Commentaries. Nashville: Abingdon, 2003.

————. *From Darkness to Light: Aspects of Conversion in the New Testament*. Overtures to Biblical Theology 20. Philadelphia: Fortress, 1986.

————. "Theology and Ecclesiology in the Miletus Speech: Reflections on Content and Context." *New Testament Studies* 50, no. 1 (January 2004): 36-52.

————. "Toward a Theology of Acts: Reading and Rereading." *Interpretation* 42, no. 2 (April 1988): 146-57.

————. "What Ever Happened to Those Prophesying Daughters?" In *A Feminist Companion to the Acts of the Apostles*, ed. A.-J. Levine with M. Blickenstaff, 49-60. Cleveland, OH: Pilgrim, 2004.

Gill, David W. J., and Conrad Gempf, eds. *The Book of Acts in Its Graeco-Roman Setting*. The Book of Acts in Its First Century Setting 2. Grand Rapids: Eerdmans, 1994.

Goodenough, Erwin R. "The Perspective of Acts." In *Studies in Luke-Acts*, ed. L. E. Keck and J. L. Martyn, 51-59. Philadelphia: Fortress, 1980.

Gowler, David B. *Host, Guest, Enemy, and Friend: Portraits of the Pharisees in Luke and Acts*. Emory Studies in Early Christianity 2. New York: Peter Lang, 1991.

Green, Joel B. "'In Our Own Languages': Pentecost, Babel, and the Shaping of Christian Community in Acts 2:1-13." In *The Word Leaps the Gap: Essays on Scripture and Theology in Honor of Richard B. Hays*, ed. J. R. Wagner, C. K. Rowe, and A. K. Grieb, 198-213. Grand Rapids: Eerdmans, 2008.

————. "Salvation to the End of the Earth: God as the Saviour in the Acts of the Apostles." In *Witness to the Gospel: The Theology of Acts*, ed. I. H.

Marshall and D. Peterson, 83-106. Grand Rapids: Eerdmans, 1998.

Gregory, Andrew F. "The Reception of Luke and Acts and the Unity of Luke-Acts." In *Rethinking the Unity and Reception of Luke and Acts*, ed. A. F. Gregory and C. K. Rowe, 82-93. Columbia, SC: University of South Carolina Press, 2010.

———. *The Reception of Luke and Acts in the Period before Irenaeus: Looking for Luke in the Second Century*. Wissenschaftliche Untersuchungen zum Neuen Testament 2. Reihe 169. Tübingen, DEU: Mohr Siebeck, 2003.

Haenchen, Ernst. *The Acts of the Apostles: A Commentary*. Translated by B. Noble and G. Shinn. Philadelphia: Westminster, 1971.

Hamm, Dennis. "Paul's Blindness and Its Healing: Clues to Symbolic Intent (Acts 9, 22 and 26)." *Biblica* 71, no. 1 (1990): 63-72.

Harnack, Adolf. *The Acts of the Apostles*. Crown Theological Library. New York: G. P. Putnam's Sons, 1909.

Harrill, J. Albert. "Divine Judgment against Ananias and Sapphira (Acts 5:1-11): A Stock Scene of Perjury and Death." *Journal of Biblical Literature* 130, no. 2 (2011): 351-69.

———. "The Dramatic Function of the Running Slave Rhoda (Acts 12.13-16): A Piece of Greco-Roman Comedy." *New Testament Studies* 46, no. 1 (2000): 150-57.

Havelaar, Henriette. "Hellenistic Parallels to Acts 5.1-11 and the Problem of Conflicting Interpretations." *Journal for the Study of the New Testament* 67 (1997): 63-82.

Hedrick, Charles W. "Paul's Conversion/Call: A Comparative Analysis of the Three Reports in Acts." *Journal of Biblical Literature* 100, no. 3 (September 1981): 415-32.

Hemer, Colin J. *The Book of Acts in the Setting of Hellenistic History*. Winona Lake, IN: Eisenbrauns, 1990.

Hengel, Martin. *Acts and the History of Earliest Christianity*. Translated by J. Bowden. Philadelphia: Fortress, 1979.

Hillard, T. W., Alanna Nobbs, and Bruce W. Winter. "Acts and the Pauline Corpus I: Ancient Literary Parallels." In *The Book of Acts in Its Ancient Literary Setting*, ed. B. W. Winter and A. D. Clarke, 183-213. The Book of Acts in Its First Century Setting 1. Grand Rapids: Eerdmans, 1993.

Holladay, Carl R. *Acts: A Commentary*. The New Testament Library. Louisville, KY: Westminster/John Knox, 2016.

Horsley, G. H. R. "Speeches and Dialogue in Acts." *New Testament Studies* 32 (1986): 609-14.

Humphrey, Edith M. "Collision of Modes?—Vision and Determining Argument in Acts 10:1–11:18." *Semeia* 71 (1995): 65-84.

Jervell, Jacob. "The Church of Jews and Godfearers." In *Luke-Acts and the Jewish People: Eight Critical Perspectives*, ed. J. B. Tyson, 11-20. Minneapolis: Augsburg, 1988.

————. *Die Apostelgeschichte: Übersetzt und erklärt*. Kritisch-exegetischer Kommentar über das Neue Testament. Göttingen, DEU: Vandenhoeck und Ruprecht, 1998.

————. *Luke and the People of God: A New Look at Luke-Acts*. Minneapolis: Augsburg, 1972.

————. *The Theology of the Acts of the Apostles*. Cambridge, UK: Cambridge University Press, 1996.

————. *The Unknown Paul: Essays on Luke-Acts and Early Christian History*. Minneapolis: Augsburg, 1984.

Johnson, Luke Timothy. *The Acts of the Apostles*. Sacra Pagina Series 5. Collegeville, MN: Liturgical, 1992.

————. *The Literary Function of Possessions in Luke-Acts*. Society of Biblical Literature Dissertation Series 39. Missoula, MT: Scholars, 1977.

————. *Living Jesus: Learning the Heart of the Gospel*. San Francisco: HarperSanFrancisco, 1999.

————. *Prophetic Jesus, Prophetic Church: The Challenge of Luke-Acts to Contemporary Christians*. Grand Rapids: Eerdmans, 2011.

————. *Sharing Possessions: Mandate and Symbol of Faith*. Overtures to Biblical Theology 9. Philadelphia: Fortress, 1981.

Juel, Donald. *Luke-Acts: The Promise of History*. Atlanta: John Knox, 1983.

Kartzow, Marianne B., and Halvor Moxnes. "Complex Identities: Ethnicity, Gender and Religion in the Story of the Ethiopian Eunuch (Acts 8:26-40)." *Religion and Theology* 17 (2010): 184-204.

Keck, Leander E., and J. Louis Martyn, eds. *Studies in Luke-Acts*. Philadelphia: Fortress, 1980.

Keener, Craig S. *Acts: An Exegetical Commentary*. 4 vols. Grand Rapids: Baker Academic, 2012-15.

Kilgallen, John J. "The Speech of Stephen, Acts 7:2-53." *The Expository Times* 115, no. 9 (June 2004): 293-97.

Knox, John. *Chapters in a Life of Paul*. Rev. ed. Macon, GA: Mercer University Press, 1987.

————. *Marcion and the New Testament: An Essay in the Early History of the Canon*. Chicago: University of Chicago Press, 1942.

Kremer, Jacob, ed. *Les Actes des Apôtres: Traditions, rédaction, théologie*. Bibliotheca ephemeridum theologicarum lovaniensium 48. Leuven, BEL: Leuven University Press, 1979.

Krodel, Gerhard A. *Acts*. Augsburg Commentary on the New Testament. Minneapolis: Augsburg, 1986.

Kurz, William S. "Narrative Models for Imitation in Luke-Acts." In *Greeks, Romans, and Christians: Essays in Honor of Abraham J. Malherbe*, ed. D. L. Balch, E. Ferguson, and W. Meeks, 171-89. Minneapolis: Fortress, 1990.

————. *Reading Luke-Acts: Dynamics of Biblical Narrative*. Louisville, KY: Westminster/John Knox, 1993.

Lake, Kirsopp. "The Apostolic Council in Jerusalem." In *Additional Notes to the Commentary on Acts*, ed. K. Lake and H. J. Cadbury, 195-99. Vol. 5 of *The Acts of the Apostles*, ed. F. J. Foakes-Jackson and K. Lake. The Beginnings of Christianity 1. London: Macmillan, 1933.

————. "The Communism of Acts II. and IV.–V. and the Appointment of the Seven." In *Additional Notes to the Commentary on Acts*, ed. K. Lake and H. J. Cadbury, 140-51. Vol. 5 of *The Acts of the Apostles*, ed. F. J. Foakes-Jackson and K. Lake. The Beginnings of Christianity 1. London: Macmillan, 1933.

Larkin, William J., Jr. *Acts*. The IVP New Testament Commentary Series 5. Downers Grove, IL: InterVarsity, 1995.

Lentz, John Clayton, Jr. *Luke's Portrait of Paul*. Society for New Testament Studies Monograph Series 77. Cambridge, UK: Cambridge University Press, 1993.

Levine, Amy-Jill, ed., with Marianne Blickenstaff. *A Feminist Companion to the Acts of the Apostles*. Cleveland: Pilgrim, 2004.

Levinskaya, Irina. *The Book of Acts in Its Diaspora Setting*. The Book of Acts in Its First Century Setting 5. Grand Rapids: Eerdmans, 1996.

Levinsohn, Stephen H. *Textual Connections in Acts*. Society of Biblical Literature Monograph Series 31. Atlanta: Scholars, 1987.

Litwak, Kenneth D. *Echoes of Scripture in Luke-Acts: Telling the History of God's People Intertextually*. Journal for the Study of the New Testament: Supplement Series 282. New York: T. and T. Clark, 2005.

Lohfink, Gerhard. *Die Sammlung Israels: Eine Untersuchung zur lukanischen Ekklesiologie*. Studien zum Alten und Neuen Testaments 39. München, DEU: Kösel, 1975.

Longenecker, Richard N. "The Acts of the Apostles." In vol. 9 of *The Expositor's Bible Commentary*, 205-573. 12 vols. Edited by F. E. Gaebelein. Grand Rapids: Zondervan, 1981.

————. *Galatians*. Word Biblical Commentary 41. Dallas: Word, 1990.

Löning, Karl. "Das Verhältnis zum Judentum als Identitätsproblem der Kirche nach der Apostelgeschichte." In *"Ihr alle aber seid Brüder": Festschrift für A. Th. Khoury zum 60. Geburtstag*, ed. L. Hagemann and E. Pulsfort, 304-19. Würzburg, DEU: Echter, 1990.

Lüdemann, Gerd. *Early Christianity according to the Traditions in Acts: A Commentary*. Translated by J. Bowden. Minneapolis: Fortress, 1989.

————. *Opposition to Paul in Jewish Christianity.* Translated by M. E. Boring. Minneapolis: Fortress, 1989.

Lyons, George. *Galatians: A Commentary in the Wesleyan Tradition.* New Beacon Bible Commentary. Kansas City: Beacon Hill Press of Kansas City, 2012.

MacDonald, Dennis R. "Paul's Farewell to the Ephesian Elders and Hector's Farewell to Andromache: A Strategic Imitation of Homer's *Iliad.*" In *Contextualizing Acts: Lukan Narrative and Greco-Roman Discourse,* ed. T. Penner and C. V. Stichele, 189-203. Atlanta: Society of Biblical Literature, 2003.

————. "The Shipwrecks of Odysseus and Paul." *New Testament Studies* 45 (1999): 88-107.

Maddox, Randy L. *Responsible Grace: John Wesley's Practical Theology.* Nashville: Kingswood, 1994.

Maddox, Robert. *The Purpose of Luke-Acts.* Forschungen zur Religion und Literatur des Alten und Neuen Testaments 126. Gottingen, DEU: Vandenhoeck und Ruprecht, 1982.

Malina, Bruce J. *The New Testament World: Insights from Cultural Anthropology.* Atlanta: John Knox, 1981.

Malina, Bruce J., and Jerome H. Neyrey. "Conflict in Luke-Acts: Labelling and Deviance Theory." In *The Social World of Luke-Acts: Models for Interpretation,* ed. J. H. Neyrey, 97-122. Peabody, MA: Hendrickson, 1991.

————. "Honor and Shame in Luke-Acts: Pivotal Values of the Mediterranean World." In *The Social World of Luke-Acts: Models for Interpretation,* ed. J. H. Neyrey, 25-65. Peabody, MA: Hendrickson, 1991.

Malina, Bruce J., and John J. Pilch. *Social-Science Commentary on the Book of Acts.* Minneapolis: Fortress, 2008.

Marguerat, Daniel. "La mort d'Ananias et Saphira (Ac 5.1-11) dans la stratégie narrative de Luc." *New Testament Studies* 39 (1993): 209-26.

Marin, Louis. "Essai d'analyse structurale d'Actes 10:1–11:18." *Recherches de science religieuse* 58 (1970): 39-61.

Marshall, I. Howard. *The Acts of the Apostles*. Tyndale New Testament Commentaries. Grand Rapids: Eerdmans, 1980.

———. "How Does One Write on the Theology of Acts?" In *Witness to the Gospel: The Theology of Acts*, ed. I. H. Marshall and D. Peterson, 3-16. Grand Rapids: Eerdmans, 1998.

———. *Luke: Historian and Theologian*. Grand Rapids: Zondervan, 1970.

Marshall, I. Howard, and David Peterson, eds. *Witness to the Gospel: The Theology of Acts*. Grand Rapids: Eerdmans, 1998.

Martin, Francis, ed. *Acts*. Ancient Christian Commentary on Scripture. Downers Grove, IL: InterVarsity, 2006.

Martyn, J. Louis. *Galatians: A New Translation with Introduction and Commentary*. The Anchor Bible 33A. New York: Doubleday, 1997.

Matthews, Shelly. *Perfect Martyr: The Stoning of Stephen and the Construction of Christian Identity*. New York: Oxford University Press, 2010.

Mealand, David. "Community of Goods and Utopian Allusions in Acts II–IV." *Journal of Theological Studies* 28 (1977): 96-99.

Metzger, Bruce M. *A Textual Commentary on the Greek New Testament*, 2nd ed. New York: United Bible Societies, 1994.

Mitchell, Alan C. "The Social Function of Friendship in Acts 2:44-47 and 4:32-37." *Journal of Biblical Literature* 111 (1992): 255-72.

Moessner, David P., ed. *Jesus and the Heritage of Israel: Luke's Narrative Claim upon Israel's Legacy*. Harrisburg, PA: Trinity, 1999.

———. "Paul in Acts: Preacher of Eschatological Repentance to Israel." *New Testament Studies* 34 (1988): 96-104.

Moreland, Milton. "The Jerusalem Community in Acts: Mythmaking and the Sociorhetorical Functions of a Lukan Setting." In *Contextualizing Acts: Lukan Narrative and Greco-Roman Discourse*, ed. T. Penner and C. Vander Stichele, 285-310. Atlanta: Society of Biblical Literature, 2003.

Moule, C. F. D. "The Christology of Acts." In *Studies in Luke-Acts*, ed. L. E. Keck and J. L. Martyn, 159-85. Philadelphia: Fortress, 1980.

Moxnes, Halvor. "Patron-Client Relations and the New Community in Luke-Acts." In *The Social World of Luke-Acts: Models for Interpretation*, ed. J. H. Neyrey, 241-68. Peabody, MA: Hendrickson, 1991.

Neil, William. *Acts.* New Century Bible Commentary. Grand Rapids: Eerdmans, 1973.

Neyrey, Jerome H., ed. *The Social World of Luke-Acts: Models for Interpretation.* Peabody, MA: Hendrickson, 1991.

Nolland, John. "A Fresh Look at Acts 15.10." *New Testament Studies* 27 (1980): 105-15.

O'Toole, R. F. "Why Did Luke Write Acts (Lk-Acts)?" *Biblical Theology Bulletin* 7 (1977): 66-76.

Oropeza, B. J. *In the Footsteps of Judas and Other Defectors: The Gospels, Acts, and Johannine Letters.* Apostasy in the New Testament Communities 1. Eugene, OR: Cascade, 2011.

Painter, John. *Just James: The Brother of Jesus in History and Tradition.* 2nd ed. Studies on Personalities of the New Testament. Columbia, SC: University of South Carolina Press, 2004.

Palmer, Darryl W. "Acts and the Ancient Historical Monograph." In *The Book of Acts in Its Ancient Literary Setting*, ed. B. W. Winter and A. D. Clarke, 1-30. The Book of Acts in Its First Century Setting 1. Grand Rapids: Eerdmans, 1993.

Panagopoulos, Johannes. "Zur Theologie der Apostelgeschichte." *Novum Testamentum* 14 (1972): 137-59.

Parsons, Mikeal C. *Acts.* Paideia Commentaries on the New Testament. Grand Rapids: Baker Academic, 2008.

———. *Body and Character in Luke and Acts: The Subversion of Physiognomy in Early Christianity.* Grand Rapids: Baker Academic, 2006.

Parsons, Mikeal C., and Joseph B. Tyson, eds. *Cadbury, Knox, and Talbert: American Contributions to the Study of Acts.* Atlanta: Scholars, 1992.

Parsons, Mikeal C., and Richard I. Pervo. *Rethinking the Unity of Luke and Acts.* Minneapolis: Fortress, 1993.

Penner, Todd. "Civilizing Discourse: Acts, Declamation, and the Rhetoric of the *Polis*." In *Contextualizing Acts: Lukan Narrative and Greco-Roman Discourse*, ed. T. Penner and C. Vander Stichele, 65-104. Society of Biblical Literature Symposium Series 20. Atlanta: Society of Biblical Literature, 2003.

Penner, Todd, and Caroline Vander Stichele, eds. *Contextualizing Acts: Lukan Narrative and Greco-Roman Discourse*. Society of Biblical Literature Symposium Series 20. Atlanta: Society of Biblical Literature, 2003.

Perrot, Charles. "Les décisions de l'assemblée de Jérusalem." *Recherches de science religieuse* 69 (1981): 195-208.

Pervo, Richard I. *Acts: A Commentary*. Hermeneia. Minneapolis: Fortress, 2009.

———. *Dating Acts: Between the Evangelists and the Apologists*. Santa Rosa, CA: Polebridge, 2006.

———. *Luke's Story of Paul*. Minneapolis: Fortress, 1990.

———. *Profit with Delight: The Literary Genre of the Acts of the Apostles*. Philadelphia: Fortress, 1987.

Pesch, Rudolf. *Die Apostelgeschichte*. 2 vols. Evangelisch-katholischer Kommentar zum Neuen Testament 5. Zürich: Neukirchener Verlag, 1986.

Peterson, David G. *The Acts of the Apostles*. Pillar New Testament Commentary. Grand Rapids: Eerdmans, 2009.

———. "The Motif of Fulfilment and the Purpose of Luke-Acts." In *The Book of Acts in Its Ancient Literary Setting*, ed. B. W. Winter and A. D. Clarke, 83-104. The Book of Acts in Its First Century Setting 1. Grand Rapids: Eerdmans, 1993.

———. "The Worship of the New Community." In *Witness to the Gospel: The Theology of Acts*, ed. I. H. Marshall and D. Peterson, 373-96. Grand Rapids: Eerdmans, 1998.

Phillips, Thomas E., ed. *Acts and Ethics*. New Testament Monographs 9. Sheffield, UK: Sheffield Phoenix, 2005.

———. "The Genre of Acts: Moving toward a Consensus?" *Currents in Biblical Research* 4, no. 3 (2006): 365-96.

————. *Paul, His Letters, and Acts*. Library of Pauline Studies. Peabody, MA: Hendrickson, 2009.

Plümacher, Eckhard. "Die Apostelgeschichte als historische Monographie." In *Les Actes des Apôtres: Traditions, rédaction, théologie*, ed. J. Kremer, 457-66. Bibliotheca ephemeridum theologicarum lovaniensium 48. Leuven, BEL: Leuven University Press, 1979.

————. *Lukas als hellenistischer Schriftsteller: Studien zur Apostelgeschichte*. Studien zur Umwelt des Neuen Testaments 9. Göttingen, DEU: Vandenhoeck und Ruprecht, 1972.

Polhill, John B. *Acts*. The New American Commentary. Nashville: Broadman and Holman, 1992.

Porter, Stanley E. *Paul in Acts*. Library of Pauline Studies. Peabody, MA: Hendrickson, 2001.

Powell, Mark Allan. *What Are They Saying about Acts?* New York: Paulist, 1991.

Praeder, Susan M. "Luke-Acts and the Ancient Novel." In *Society of Biblical Literature: 1981 Seminar Papers*, ed. K. H. Richards, 269-92. Missoula, MT: Scholars, 1981.

Radl, Walter. *Paulus und Jesus im lukanischen Doppelwerk: Untersuchungen zu Parallelmotiven im Lukasevangelium und in der Apostelgeschichte*. Europäische Hochschulschriften. Frankfurt: Peter Lang, 1975.

Rapske, Brian M. "Opposition to the Plan of God and Persecution." In *Witness to the Gospel: The Theology of Acts*, ed. I. H. Marshall and D. Peterson, 235-56. Grand Rapids: Eerdmans, 1998.

Reimer, Ivoni Richter. *Women in the Acts of the Apostles: A Feminist Liberation Perspective*. Translated by L. M. Maloney. Minneapolis: Fortress, 1995.

Reinhardt, Wolfgang. "The Population Size of Jerusalem and the Numerical Growth of the Jerusalem Church." In *The Book of Acts in Its Palestinian Setting*, ed. R. Bauckham, 237-65. The Book of Acts in Its First Century Setting 4. Grand Rapids: Eerdmans, 1995.

Richard, Earl. "The Divine Purpose: The Jews and the Gentile Mission (Acts 15)." In *Luke-Acts: New Perspectives from the Society of Biblical Literature Seminar*, ed. C. H. Talbert, 188-209. New York: Crossroad, 1984.

Riesner, Rainer. "James's Speech (Acts 15:13-21), Simeon's Hymn (Luke 2:29-32), and Luke's Sources." In *Jesus of Nazareth: Lord and Christ; Essays on the Historical Jesus and New Testament Christology*, ed. J. B. Green and M. Turner, 263-78. Grand Rapids: Eerdmans, 1994.

Roloff, Jürgen. *Die Apostelgeschichte*. Das Neue Testament Deutsch 5. Göttingen, DEU: Vandenhoeck und Ruprecht, 1981.

Rosner, Brian S. "Acts and Biblical History." In *The Book of Acts in Its Ancient Literary Setting*, ed. B. W. Winter and A. D. Clarke, 65-82. The Book of Acts in Its First Century Setting 1. Grand Rapids: Eerdmans, 1993.

———. "The Progress of the Word." In *Witness to the Gospel: The Theology of Acts*, ed. I. H. Marshall and D. Peterson, 215-34. Grand Rapids: Eerdmans, 1998.

Rowe, C. Kavin. "Acts 2.36 and the Continuity of Lukan Christology." *New Testament Studies* 53, no. 1 (2007): 37-56.

———. *World Upside Down: Reading Acts in the Graeco-Roman Age*. New York: Oxford University Press, 2009.

Salmon, Marilyn. "Insider or Outsider? Luke's Relationship with Judaism." In *Luke-Acts and the Jewish People: Eight Critical Perspectives*, ed. J. B. Tyson, 76-82. Minneapolis: Augsburg, 1988.

Sanders, Jack T. *The Jews in Luke-Acts*. Philadelphia: Fortress, 1987.

———. "Who Is a Jew and Who Is a Gentile in the Book of Acts?" *New Testament Studies* 37 (1991): 434-55.

Schille, Gottfried. *Die Apostelgeschichte des Lukas*. Theologischer Handkommentar zum Neuen Testament 5. Berlin: Evangelische Verlagsanstalt, 1983.

Schlatter, Adolf. *Die Apostelgeschichte*. Erläuterungen zum Neuen Testament 4. Stuttgart, DEU: Calwer Verlag, 1948.

Schmidt, Daryl. "The Historiography of Acts: Deuteronomistic or Hellenistic?" In *Society of Biblical Literature: 1985 Seminar Papers*, ed. K. H. Richards, 417-27. Atlanta: Scholars, 1985.

Schmithals, Walter. *Die Apostelgeschichte des Lukas*. Zürcher Bibelkommentare. Zürich: Theologischer Verlag, 1982.

Schnabel, Eckhard J. *Acts*. Zondervan Exegetical Commentary on the New Testament. Grand Rapids: Zondervan, 2012.

Schneider, Gerhard. *Die Apostelgeschichte 1–8*. Herders theologischer Kommentar zum Neuen Testament 5. Freiburg: Herder, 1980.

———. *Die Apostelgeschichte 9–28*. Herders theologischer Kommentar zum Neuen Testament 5. Freiburg: Herder, 1982.

———. *Lukas, Theologe der Heilsgeschichte: Aufsätze zum lukanischen Doppelwerk*. Bonner biblische Beiträge 59. Königstein: Peter Hanstein, 1985.

Schweizer, Eduard. "Concerning the Speeches in Acts." In *Studies in Luke-Acts*, ed. L. E. Keck and J. L. Martyn, 208-16. Philadelphia: Fortress, 1980.

Scott, J. Julius, Jr. "The Cornelius Incident in the Light of Its Jewish Setting." *Journal of the Evangelical Theological Society* 34, no. 4 (1991): 475-84.

Seccombe, David. "The New People of God." In *Witness to the Gospel: The Theology of Acts*, ed. I. H. Marshall and D. Peterson, 349-72. Grand Rapids: Eerdmans, 1998.

Seifrid, M. A. "Jesus and the Law in Acts." *Journal for the Study of the New Testament* 30 (1987): 39-57.

Seim, Turid Karlsen. *The Double Message: Patterns of Gender in Luke and Acts*. Nashville: Abingdon, 1994.

Shauf, Scott. "Locating the Eunuch: Characterization and Narrative Context in Acts 8:26-40." *Catholic Biblical Quarterly* 71, no. 4 (2009): 762-75.

Sheeley, Steven M. "Narrative Asides and Narrative Authority in Luke-Acts." *Biblical Theology Bulletin* 18 (1988): 102-7.

———. *Narrative Asides in Luke-Acts*. Journal for the Study of the New Testament: Supplement Series 72. Sheffield, UK: JSOT, 1992.

Shepherd, William H., Jr. *The Narrative Function of the Holy Spirit as a Character in Luke-Acts*. Society of Biblical Literature Dissertation Series 147. Atlanta: Scholars, 1994.

Slingerland, Dixon. "Acts 18:1-18, the Gallio Inscription, and Absolute Pauline Chronology." *Journal of Biblical Literature* 110, no. 3 (1991): 439-49.

———. "'The Jews' in the Pauline Portion of Acts." *Journal of the American Academy of Religion* 54, no. 2 (1986): 305-21.

Soards, Marion L. *The Speeches in Acts: Their Content, Context, and Concerns.* Louisville, KY: Westminster/John Knox, 1994.

Spencer, F. Scott. "The Ethiopian Eunuch and His Bible: A Social-Science Analysis." *Biblical Theology Bulletin* 22, no. 4 (Winter 1992): 155-65.

———. *Journeying through Acts: A Literary-Critical Reading.* Peabody, MA: Hendrickson, 2004.

———. "Out of Mind, Out of Voice: Slave-Girls and Prophetic Daughters in Luke-Acts." *Biblical Interpretation* 7, no. 2 (April 1999): 133-55.

———. "Scared to Death: The Rhetoric of Fear in the 'Tragedy' of Ananias and Sapphira." In *Reading Acts Today: Essays in Honour of Loveday C. A. Alexander*, ed. S. Walton, T. E. Phillips, L. K. Pietersen, and F. S. Spencer, 63-80. London: T. and T. Clark, 2011.

Squires, John T. "The Plan of God." In *Witness to the Gospel: The Theology of Acts*, ed. I. H. Marshall and D. Peterson, 19-39. Grand Rapids: Eerdmans, 1998.

———. *The Plan of God in Luke-Acts.* Society for New Testament Studies Monograph Series 76. Cambridge, UK: Cambridge University Press, 1993.

Stegemann, Wolfgang. *Zwischen Synagoge und Obrigkeit: Zur historischen Situation der lukanischen Christen.* Forschungen zur Religion und Literatur des Alten und Neuen Testaments 152. Göttingen, DEU: Vandenhoeck und Ruprecht, 1991.

Sterling, Gregory E. "'Athletes of Virtue': An Analysis of the Summaries in Acts (2:41-47; 4:32-35; 5:12-16)." *Journal of Biblical Literature* 113, no. 4 (1994): 679-96.

———. *Historiography and Self-Definition: Josephos, Luke-Acts, and Apologetic Historiography.* Leiden, NL: Brill, 1992.

Sternberg, Meir. *The Poetics of Biblical Narrative: Ideological Literature and the Drama of Reading.* Bloomington, IN: Indiana University Press, 1985.

Strelan, Rick. "The Running Prophet (Acts 8:30)." *Novum Testamentum* 43, no. 1 (2001): 31-38.

Talbert, Charles H. *Literary Patterns, Theological Themes, and the Genre of Luke-Acts.* Society of Biblical Literature Monograph Series 20. Missoula, MT: Scholars, 1974.

———, ed. *Luke-Acts: New Perspectives from the Society of Biblical Literature Seminar.* New York: Crossroad, 1984.

———. *Reading Acts: A Literary and Theological Commentary on the Acts of the Apostles.* Reading the New Testament. New York: Crossroad, 1997.

Tannehill, Robert C. "Israel in Luke-Acts: A Tragic Story." *Journal of Biblical Literature* 104, no. 1 (1985): 69-85.

———. *The Narrative Unity of Luke-Acts: A Literary Interpretation.* Vol. 2, *The Acts of the Apostles.* Minneapolis: Fortress, 1990.

———. "Rejection by Jews and Turning to Gentiles: The Pattern of Paul's Mission in Acts." In *Luke-Acts and the Jewish People: Eight Critical Perspectives,* ed. J. B. Tyson, 83-101. Minneapolis: Augsburg, 1988.

Thompson, Richard P. *Acts: A Commentary in the Wesleyan Tradition.* New Beacon Bible Commentary. Kansas City: Beacon Hill Press of Kansas City, 2015.

———. "Believers and Religious Leaders in Jerusalem: Contrasting Portraits of Jews in Acts 1–7." In *Literary Studies in Luke-Acts: Essays in Honor of Joseph B. Tyson,* ed. R. P. Thompson and T. E. Phillips, 327-44. Macon, GA: Mercer University Press, 1998.

———. *Keeping the Church in Its Place: The Church as Narrative Character in Acts.* New York: T. and T. Clark, 2006.

———. "'Say It Ain't So, Paul!': The Accusations against Paul in Acts 21 in the Light of His Ministry in Acts 16–20." *Biblical Research* 45 (2000): 34-50.

———. "'What Do You Think You Are Doing, Paul?' Synagogues, Ministry, and Ethics in Acts 16–21." In *Acts and Ethics,* ed. T. E. Phillips, 64-78. Sheffield, UK: Sheffield Phoenix, 2005.

Thompson, Richard P., and Thomas E. Phillips, eds. *Literary Studies in Luke-Acts: Essays in Honor of Joseph B. Tyson*. Macon, GA: Mercer University Press, 1998.

Tiede, David L. "Acts 11:1-18." *Interpretation* 42, no. 2 (1988): 175-79.

———. "'Glory to Thy People Israel': Luke-Acts and the Jews." In *Luke-Acts and the Jewish People: Eight Critical Perspectives*, ed. J. B. Tyson, 21-34. Minneapolis: Augsburg, 1988.

Towner, Philip H. "Mission Practice and Theology under Construction (Acts 18–20)." In *Witness to the Gospel: The Theology of Acts*, ed. I. H. Marshall and D. Peterson, 417-36. Grand Rapids: Eerdmans, 1998.

Turner, Max. "The 'Spirit of Prophecy' as the Power of Israel's Restoration and Witness." In *Witness to the Gospel: The Theology of Acts*, ed. I. H. Marshall and D. Peterson, 327-48. Grand Rapids: Eerdmans, 1998.

Twelftree, Graham H. *People of the Spirit: Exploring Luke's View of the Church*. Grand Rapids: Baker Academic, 2009.

Tyson, Joseph B. "The Emerging Church and the Problem of Authority in Acts." *Interpretation* 42, no. 2 (1988): 132-45.

———. *Images of Judaism in Luke-Acts*. Columbia, SC: University of South Carolina Press, 1992.

———. "The Jewish Public in Luke-Acts." *New Testament Studies* 30, no. 4 (1984): 574-83.

———. "Jews and Judaism in Luke-Acts: Reading as a Godfearer." *New Testament Studies* 41 (1995): 19-38.

———, ed. *Luke-Acts and the Jewish People: Eight Critical Perspectives*. Minneapolis: Augsburg, 1988.

———. *Marcion and Luke-Acts: A Defining Struggle*. Columbia, SC: University of South Carolina Press, 2006.

———. "The Problem of Jewish Rejection in Acts." In *Luke-Acts and the Jewish People: Eight Critical Perspectives*, ed. J. B. Tyson, 124-37. Minneapolis: Augsburg, 1988.

van der Horst, Pieter W. "Hellenistic Parallels to the Acts of the Apostles (2.1-47)." *Journal for the Study of the New Testament* 25 (1985): 49-60.

van de Sandt, Huub. "An Explanation of Acts 15.6-21 in the Light of Deuteronomy 4.29-35 (LXX)." *Journal for the Study of the New Testament* 46 (1992): 73-97.

van Unnik, W. C. "Luke's Second Book and the Rules of Hellenistic Historiography." In *Les Actes des Apôtres: Traditions, rédaction, théologie*, ed. J. Kremer, 37-60. Bibliotheca ephemeridum theologicarum lovaniensium 48. Leuven, BEL: Leuven University Press, 1979.

Vielhauer, Philipp. "On the 'Paulinism' of Acts." In *Studies in Luke-Acts*, ed. L. E. Keck and J. L. Martyn, 33-50. Philadelphia: Fortress, 1980.

Wagner, J. Ross, C. Kavin Rowe, and A. Katherine Grieb, eds. *The Word Leaps the Gap: Essays on Scripture and Theology in Honor of Richard B. Hays.* Grand Rapids: Eerdmans, 2008.

Walker, William O., Jr. "Acts and the Pauline Corpus Revisited: Peter's Speech at the Jerusalem Conference." In *Literary Studies in Luke-Acts: Essays in Honor of Joseph B. Tyson*, ed. R. P. Thompson and T. E. Phillips, 77-86. Macon, GA: Mercer University Press, 1998.

Wall, Robert W. "The Acts of the Apostles: Introduction, Commentary, and Reflections." In vol. 10 of *The New Interpreter's Bible*, 3-368. 12 vols. Edited by L. Keck. Nashville: Abingdon, 2002.

Wedderburn, A. J. M. "The 'Apostolic Decree': Tradition and Redaction." *Novum Testamentum* 35, no. 4 (1993): 362-89.

———. "Traditions and Redaction in Acts 2:1-13." *Journal for the Study of the New Testament* 55 (1994): 27-54.

Weiser, Alfons. *Die Apostelgeschichte.* 2 vols. Ökumenischer Taschenbuchkommentar zum Neuen Testament. Würzburg, DEU: Echter, 1986.

———. "Das 'Apostelkonzil' (Apg 15,1-35): Ereignis, Überlieferung, lukanische Deutung." *Biblische Zeitschrift* 28 (1984): 145-67.

Wenham, David. "Acts and the Pauline Corpus." In *The Book of Acts in Its Ancient Literary Setting*, ed. B. W. Winter and A. D. Clarke, 215-58. The Book of Acts in Its First Century Setting 1. Grand Rapids: Eerdmans, 1993.

Wesley, John. *Explanatory Notes upon the New Testament.* London: Epworth, 1958.

Wilcox, Max. "The 'God-Fearers' in Acts—A Reconsideration." *Journal for the Study of the New Testament* 13 (1981): 102-22.

Williams, David John. *Acts.* New International Biblical Commentary 5. Peabody, MA: Hendrickson, 1990.

Wills, Lawrence M. "The Depiction of the Jews in Acts." *Journal of Biblical Literature* 110, no. 4 (1991): 631-54.

Wilson, Brittany E. "'Neither Male nor Female': The Ethiopian Eunuch in Acts 8.26-40." *New Testament Studies* 60, no. 3 (2014): 403-22.

Wilson, Stephen G. *The Gentiles and the Gentile Mission in Luke-Acts.* Society for New Testament Studies Monograph Series 23. Cambridge, UK: Cambridge University Press, 1973.

————. *Luke and the Law.* Society for New Testament Studies Monograph Series 50. Cambridge, UK: Cambridge University Press, 1983.

Winter, Bruce W., and Andrew D. Clarke, eds. *The Book of Acts in Its Ancient Literary Setting.* The Book of Acts in Its First Century Setting 1. Grand Rapids: Eerdmans, 1993.

Witherington, Ben, III. *The Acts of the Apostles: A Socio-Rhetorical Commentary.* Grand Rapids: Eerdmans, 1998.

Witherup, Ronald D. "Cornelius Over and Over and Over Again: 'Functional Redundancy' in the Acts of the Apostles." *Journal for the Study of the New Testament* 49 (1993): 45-66.

————. "Functional Redundancy in the Acts of the Apostles: A Case Study." *Journal for the Study of the New Testament* 48 (1992): 67-86.

Zettner, Christoph. *Amt, Gemeinde und kirchliche Einheit in der Apostelgeschichte des Lukas.* New York: Peter Lang, 1991.

Ziesler, J. A. "Luke and the Pharisees." *New Testament Studies* 25 (1979): 146-57.

Zingg, Paul. *Das Wachsen der Kirche: Beiträge zur Frage der lukanischen Redaktion und Theologie.* Orbis biblicus et orientalis. Göttingen, DEU: Vandenhoeck und Ruprecht, 1974.